COMPETITION IN AFRICA

Insights from key industries

Edited by

SIMON ROBERTS

in collaboration with:

African Competition Forum

Competition Authority of Botswana

Competition Authority of Kenya

Namibian Competition Commission

Competition Commission of South Africa

Fair Competition Commission of Tanzania

Competition and Consumer Protection Commission of Zambia

HSRC PRESS

Published by HSRC Press
Private Bag X9182, Cape Town 8000, South Africa
www.hsrcpress.ac.za

First published 2016

ISBN (soft cover) 978-0-7969-2545-9
ISBN (pdf) 978-0-7969-2546-6

This book has undergone a double-blind independent peer-review process overseen by the HSRC Press Editorial Board.

Copy-edited by Aré van Schalkwyk
Typeset by Nazley Samsodien
Cover design by Riaan Wilmans
Printed by Creda Communications

Distributed in Africa by Blue Weaver
Tel: +27 (0) 21 701 4477; Fax Local: +27 (0) 21 701 7302; Fax International: 0927865242139
www.blueweaver.co.za

Distributed in Europe and the United Kingdom by Eurospan Distribution Services (EDS)
Tel: +44 (0) 17 6760 4972; Fax: +44 (0) 17 6760 1640
www.eurospanbookstore.com

Distributed in North America by River North Editions, from IPG
Call toll-free: (800) 888 4741; Fax: +1 (312) 337 5985
www.ipgbook.com

Contents

Figures

Tables

Acronyms

ACP	African Caribbean, and Pacific Group of States
ADMARC	Agricultural Development Marketing Corporation
AFMA	Animal Feed Manufacturers Association
AGOA	African Growth and Opportunity Act
AISP	Agricultural Input Subsidy Programme
ARL	Agricultural Resources Ltd
ARM	Athi River Mining
BPA	Botswana Poultry Association
C&CI	Cement and Concrete Institute
CAADP	Comprehensive Africa Agricultural Development Programme
CAN	Calcium ammonium nitrate
CBH	Country Bird Holdings
CCPC	Competition and Consumer Protection Commission of Zambia
CDSA	Cement Distributors (South Africa) (Pty) Ltd
CEDA	Citizen Entrepreneurial Development Agency
CFTC	Competition and Fair Trade Commission of Malawi
CIF	Cost, insurance and freight
CLP	Corporate Leniency Policy
COMESA	Common Market for Eastern and Southern Africa
DCG	Dar es Salaam Corridor Group
DPFO	Developing Poultry Farmers Organisation
DTI	Department of Trade and Industry
EAC	East African Community
EAPCC	East African Portland Cement Company
EBA	Everything But Arms
ERC	Estimated Recoverable Crystals
ETG	Export Trading Group
EU	European Union
FISP	Farm Input Subsidy Programme (Malawi)
FISP	Fertilizer/Farmer Input Support Programmme (Zambia)
FOB	Free on Board
FRA	Food Reserve Agency
FTA	Free-trade Agreement
IDC	Industrial Development Corporation
IFDC	International Fertilizer Development Centre
IQF	Individually quick-frozen
ITAC	International Trade Administration Commission

KSB	Kenya Sugar Board
LDC	Least-developed Countries
MACO	Ministry of Agriculture and Cooperatives
MGDS	Malawi Growth and Development Strategy
NAIVS	National Agriculture Input Voucher Scheme
NPC-Cimpor	Natal Portland Cement-Cimpor
NPI	Namib Poultry Industries
NPK	Nitrogen, Phosphorus and Potassium
OPC	Ordinary Portland Cement
PAZ	Poultry Association of Zambia
PPC	Pretoria Portland Cement
RTOA	Road Transport Owners' Association
SACU	South African Customs Union
SADC	Southern African Development Community
SAPA	South African Poultry Association
SASA	South African Sugar Association
SFFRFM	Smallholder Farmers Fertilizer Revolving Fund of Malawi
SMME	Small, Medium and Micro-sized Enterprise
SUMATRA	Surface and Marine Transport and Regulatory Authority
TASGA	Tanzania Sugarcane Growers Association
TATOA	Tanzania Truck Owner's Association
TFRA	Tanzania Fertilizer Regulatory Authority
TIC	Tanzania Investment Corporation
TPC	Tanzania Portland Cement
TPC Limited	Tanganyika Planting Company Limited
VKB	Vrystaat Koöperasie Beperk
WTO	World Trade Organisation

Foreword

We are very pleased as the current and former chairpersons of the African Competition Forum (ACF) to introduce this book on Competition in Africa – Insights from Key Industries. The book is a good example of collaboration between competition authorities and researchers to understand the nature of competition challenges at the industry level. It arises from a project started under the leadership of the first ACF chairperson, Wang'ombe Kariuki. Under the direction of the current chairperson, Tembinkosi Bonakele, the work of the ACF has built on this in an ongoing programme of collaboration to develop a shared knowledge-base on competition in Africa.

The African Competition Forum is a network of competition authorities in Africa, with 35 African countries as members. It was established in 2011 to promote the adoption of competition laws, help build the capacity of new authorities, and assist in advocating for the implementation of competition reforms to the benefit of member countries. As a network, the ACF seeks to work through partnerships to strengthen knowledge and understanding within the continent, as well as globally. The projects which led to this volume are an example of such partnerships in action.

The chapters examine competition issues across countries in four very important sectors. In each of these sectors there are powerful multinational incumbent firms who, as is only to be expected, vigorously defend their conduct in light of critical scrutiny. The job of competition authorities is, however, to undertake just such scrutiny. The countries included here, Botswana, Kenya, Malawi, Namibia, South Africa, Tanzania and Zambia, all have relatively young competition authorities tasked with this work.

In this regard, it is important to emphasise that the studies which formed the basis of the chapters of this book were research exercises and not investigations. The studies were conducted by independent researchers along with staff of competition authorities and the analyses are of the teams of researchers involved. The conclusions drawn reflect the information at the time of the studies. We further wish to highlight that in some cases the companies contested the findings of the researchers. The researchers took into account the representations made where appropriate. There has also been a rigorous blind review process.

Competition authorities undertake investigations and market inquiries in which their formal powers are exercised. The issues raised by the studies have led to investigations in a number of instances and have contributed to changes in policies. Notable developments include new entry in cement which has brought higher levels of competition and investment, and has positively impacted on the costs of infrastructure and housing. There has been greater openness in sugar markets in some countries which has meant improvements in regional competitive rivalry. Increased rivalry in fertilizer transport and trading along with effective anti-cartel enforcement has reduced some of the apparently very high mark-ups in countries such as Zambia. Investments in agriculture have underpinned economic growth across most of the countries. A key challenge is for this to translate into more competitive outcomes, investment and employment in downstream activities such as poultry.

If the 'Africa rising' narrative is to lead to sustained and more inclusive growth, then markets need to be dynamic and competitive. This not only relates to competition enforcement, but areas where proactive measures can open up markets for greater participation, as pointed out in the book. The chapters emphasise the need for strong cooperation across countries as well as the importance of understanding and advocating for competition as part of a development vision for Africa. The ACF is vigorously pursuing this agenda and provides a critical platform for cooperation between agencies to achieve tangible outcomes for the people of Africa.

Wang'ombe Kariuki

First Chairperson of African Competition Forum and Director General, Competition Authority of Kenya

Tembinkosi Bonakele

Chairperson of African Competition Forum and Commissioner, Competition Commission South Africa

Acknowledgements

The support of the International Development Research Centre (IDRC) of Canada and Germany's Gesellschaft für Internationale Zusammenarbeit (GIZ) for the underlying research which formed the basis for the chapters is gratefully acknowledged. Three of the studies drawn on here were undertaken as part of an African Competition Forum project funded by the IDRC while the fourth was undertaken for the Southern African Development Community competition committee and was funded by GIZ. The funders do not bear any responsibility for the findings which are those of the authors themselves.

The project received the support of many different parties which enabled it to progress from the initial studies to this publication in this book. The African Competition Forum under the chairmanships of Wang'ombe Kariuki and Tembinkosi Bonakele has been the key sponsor all along. The Competition Commission of South Africa graciously allowed me time to work on it in the early stages while I was employed there until the end of 2012 and the University of Johannesburg has provided support thereafter. The book benefitted very substantially from the careful editing of Catherine Garson, as well as the support of the team at HSRC Press.

Simon Roberts

University of Johannesburg

1 *Competition and economic development in southern and East Africa*

Simon Roberts

The nature of competitive rivalry, and the power and interests of large firms and their owners, is at the heart of how countries develop.[1] Large firms shape the economy as they can make the investments required in productive capacity, and provide the upstream inputs and services required by smaller businesses. In many areas, these firms are also the main routes to market. At the same time, large firms tend to have market power if competition between them is weak. In crude terms, it is critical whether these firms focus on extracting rents through market power, or whether they earn returns that reward their effort, creativity and entrepreneurship.

Competition is, however, often overlooked when we consider regional integration. Recent attention on regional integration has focused on removing barriers to trade as part of 'defragmenting Africa' to overcome the legacy of colonial borders.[2] Emphasis has also been placed on constructive measures required for more meaningful and deeper integration, such as investments in improved transport infrastructure and the development of effective institutional arrangements.

It is important to remember that firms invest to supply customers in geographic markets that do not necessarily match national borders. The competitive dynamics depend on the location of production, the location of the main sources of consumption, and logistics infrastructure and costs. National borders are only a part of the picture and taking a regional view is important for understanding outcomes such as pricing, as well as the underlying competitive dynamics.

This book looks at the patterns of economic activity across southern and East Africa from a different standpoint. The chapters examine the firms responsible for production, investment and employment in key sectors. We consider the regional and international scope of the businesses, the nature of the competitive rivalry, and draw out implications for a more nuanced understanding of competition and economic development.

Understanding competition at the regional level

In industries characterised by economies of scale, relatively few firms will exist in small economies. Economies of scale mean that to achieve low average costs firms must have large production plants. Also, a small number of firms controlling production within countries and across the region implies that the level of competition between them may be low.

It is evident that the market power of large firms, whether exerted unilaterally or through coordination with each other in a cartel, harms economic development and low-income groups. Typically, it means higher prices for goods and services, which harms consumers. Where these are intermediate products and inputs such as fertilizer, there is a knock-on effect on production, making it less competitive. At the same time, we must remember that profits are the incentive to invest – the question is whether the returns being earned reflect a competitive reward on the capital invested or the advantages of an incumbent position to yield supra-competitive prices and margins.

Given the small size of many African economies, especially relative to the minimum efficient scale for industrial production, there may well be only one or two substantial producers in individual economies. These large firms may be internationalised along different dimensions, including through ownership relations, strategic partnerships and distribution arrangements. This means that a regional perspective to firm decision-making, such as that relating to investment and the location of production, is critical. In addition, while international trade allows countries to specialise in production and benefit from being able to import those goods they do not produce, if there is substantial market power and anticompetitive conduct, it follows that trade flows also transfer large profits.

The studies in this book reveal that the same large firms may operate across countries in a given industry to such an extent that trade flows could mean competing with their own subsidiaries, or trade may involve intra-firm transactions regarding inputs. Therefore, without having a regional view, it is impossible to understand how competition is, or is not, working. If we only kept our observations within countries, we would miss the bigger picture.

Anticompetitive arrangements such as cartels can have a regional and international scope. The most obvious example is a cartel that divides markets by allocating countries to different producers. In this scenario, Firm A is allocated a number of countries, Firm B a different set, and Firm C the remaining countries across the region. Each country appears to have a single supplier, but at regional level the cartel arrangement is evident, harming consumers across all the countries. This is not only a theoretical possibility. Already, these kinds of cartels have been found to be operating across countries in southern Africa in cement, concrete products and fertilizer.[3] Larger countries' markets are divided between two or three of the producers, while smaller economies are the domain of just a single supplier under the cartel agreement.

One of the challenges a cartel faces is how to monitor and maintain the agreement between its members. By raising trade barriers, governments can assist firms to protect their market power within those countries, which undermines competition at a regional level.

To sustain such supra-competitive rents it is also necessary for the incumbent firms to keep out entrants and undermine smaller rivals. In the parlance of competition policy this is about exclusionary strategies, including by a single dominant firm abusing its position of dominance. Developments in economic theory explain how a firm can protect and extend its monopoly power through a range of strategies.[4] These strategies include excluding rivals by controlling crucial inputs, supplying these inputs at high prices, and inducing customers not to buy from competitors through various tactics. Exclusionary strategies to abuse a dominant position are more likely where a firm has a very high market share, as well as where there are scale economies and information asymmetries. As we now discuss, these have important implications for developing countries.

Competition and economic development

It has been widely observed that small and developing economies are likely to have higher levels of concentration and bigger competition problems than those of Europe or North America (Brusick & Evenett 2008; Dabbah 2010; Fox 2012; Gal 2003). Scale economies therefore are that much more important, as are dynamic issues to do with the process of competitive rivalry in building production capabilities and accessing inputs and markets (Gal 2003, 2009; Sutton 2012).

Growth and development through regional integration initiatives depend on the decisions of companies to increase productive capacity and make long-term investment decisions across the region. However, if a few large companies dominate an industry and are able to extract supra-competitive profits, then the regional scope of these firms can undermine growth. Where consumers are downstream industries, any anticompetitive conduct raises costs and undermines the competitiveness of downstream firms. The existence of supra-competitive profits (or rents) from, for example, collusive conduct, further implies that the incumbent firms will lobby political interests to create barriers to entrants, including through regulations (Khan 2006).

Harm from low levels of competition (more likely in protected national economies) and the sustained earning of supra-competitive margins also includes the exclusion of rivals – typically smaller firms and entrants that are attracted by the returns to be made but whose increased participation would undermine the anticompetitive arrangements. Anticompetitive arrangements thus typically involve entrenched 'insiders' protecting their position. This has the effect of undermining participation in the economy and stifling the dynamism that comes with it, which goes far beyond simple effects on prices.

By comparison, active rivalry means improved service and product offerings, and ongoing improvements in the capabilities required to deliver these. In other words, effort and ingenuity are rewarded rather than incumbency. This can also be described as the difference between 'performance competition' through better products and 'handicap competition', which undermines rivals (Gerber 2010).

The importance of disciplining the power of large firms, ensuring more inclusive growth, and tackling limitations on access to economic activity, has been highlighted in recent contributions on growth and development (Acemoglu and Robinson 2012; North et al. 2009). Thus, while large firms are crucial to these investments, it is important that the power of such firms is disciplined by rivalry (Amsden 2003).

Economic development clearly requires investment in local productive capacity. While imports can provide more intense competition and lower prices to consumers, these benefits will not support broad-based growth in the absence of developing the productive base, such as in agriculture and agro-processing in most African countries. At the regional level, this suggests realising higher levels of competition alongside increased investment in a wider regional market where increased two-way trade between countries reflects growth in productive capacity across countries. Regional integration cannot be sustained if the investment is all in one country and the others remain large net importers. This indicates that there is a need for industrial and agricultural policies to be complementary to competition policy. What is clear is that policies that protect dominant firms or tight cartels within countries, for instance by erecting trade barriers, will neither contribute to growth nor support more competitive outcomes. Regional integration provides scope for greater competitive rivalry in a larger market, but this will not be realised if smaller economies simply become undermined by the largest regional economy.

Competition, properly located, is about the dynamic process of rivalry. There are important constructive dimensions to competition, such as enabling rival firms to bring products to market. Competition does not exist simply if there is the absence of anticompetitive arrangements. Optimal or effective competition is partly an outcome of investments in local productive capacity – to establish the competitors (Singh 2004). The ability to develop productive capabilities (such as accessing finance and key infrastructure or investing in skills) is crucial to effective competitive rivalry and has been highlighted as being at the centre of a country's economic development.[5] Inclusive growth therefore has a competition dimension, which to be properly understood, needs to be viewed at the regional level.

The links between the fields of competition, trade and regional integration, and inclusive growth generally, however, have not generally been well developed in the literature.[6] There are also critical considerations regarding policy choices about competition enforcement across countries relating to the competition regime and the institutional framework. This book seeks to make an important contribution to better understanding these issues.

Background to the book

The challenges of understanding competition at the regional level led to the African Competition Forum (ACF) of competition authorities across the continent launching a six-country research project covering the cement, poultry and sugar industries in 2012. The six countries are Botswana, Kenya, Namibia, South Africa, Tanzania and Zambia. All six countries were covered in the cement study, while the sugar and poultry studies assessed developments in four countries. The studies were carried out by teams of researchers from the different competition authorities, in some cases with assistance from external economists.[7] A fourth chapter draws from a study on fertilizer trading and transport in Malawi, Tanzania and Zambia undertaken for the Southern African Development Community (SADC).

The studies mapped out the major producers across the countries, the main changes over time and the market structures. The market dynamics were assessed, including barriers to entry, regulatory arrangements, and the outcomes observed in terms of price and supply. Issues relating to competition law that have arisen were examined, as well as the implications for competition enforcement and policy. The studies under the auspices of the ACF covered the developments up to and including 2012, with more recent notable developments being reflected.

The chapters in this book illustrate the regional scope of firms' operations and critical questions for regional economic development. In each of the industries, a few firms produce and supply across the countries studied. In the case of cement, the major firms in the region are generally associated with large multinational corporations with global reach. Similarly, in the sugar industry, the major corporations are international in scope and export to both neighbouring and deep-sea markets from the low-cost producers in the region. The poultry study reveals the expansion of companies across borders to increase the regional integration of operations. This expansion has the potential to improve the competitiveness of poultry production in southern Africa as it can enable the countries with greater agricultural potential to produce animal feed for lower-cost poultry to meet the growing consumer demand across countries. In the case of transport and trading in the fertilizer industry, the entry of suppliers from one country into another has led to higher levels of competition and significantly lower prices. Where barriers have restricted entry, prices have tended to stay higher.

The sectors that are the subject of the studies are all important in their own right. Considered together, the studies enable critical cross-cutting conclusions to be drawn, which resonate for the major questions of economic development and regional integration. The implications are the subject of the final chapter, together with reflections on the key policy agenda.

Notes

1 See, for example, Acemoglu and Robinson (2012); North et al. (2009)
2 In the words of a World Bank report (Brenton P & Isik G (2012))
3 See, for example, Makhaya et al. (2012) and Roberts S (2013)
4 See, for example, Rey & Tirole (2006)
5 See Hausmann R et al. (2007); Page J (2012); Sutton J (2004); Rodrik D (2007)
6 For example, North et al. highlight the importance of competition in moving to what they characterise as 'open access orders' as opposed to 'limited access orders', but do not analyse the key factors in competitive or uncompetitive outcomes in oligopolistic markets, implicitly assuming that in the absence of artificial barriers to entry, markets will approach perfect competition.
7 The studies were funded by the International Development Research Centre (IDRC), whose support is gratefully acknowledged. However, the IDRC bears no responsibility for the research and its findings.

References

Acemoglu D & Robinson J (2012) *Why nations fail.* New York: Random House

Amsden A (2003) *The rise of 'The rest': Challenges to the West from late-industrializing economies.* Oxford: Oxford University Press

Brenton P & Isik G (Eds) (2012) *De-fragmenting Africa: Deepening regional trade integration in goods and services.* Washington DC: World Bank

Brusick P & Evenett S (2008) Should developing countries worry about abuse of dominant power? *Wisconsin Law Review* 2, 269–294

Dabbah M (2010) Competition policy, abusive dominance and economic development: Some reflections. Paper presented at the 37th Annual Conference on International Antitrust Law and Policy, Fordham Competition Law Institute, New York, 24 September 2010

Fox E (2012) Competition, development and regional integration: In search of a competition law fit for developing countries. In J Drexl, M Bakhoum, E Fox, M Gal & D Gerber (Eds) *Competition policy and regional integration in developing countries.* Cheltenham: Edward Elgar

Gal M (2003) *Competition policy for small market economies.* Boston: Harvard University Press

Gal M (2009) Antitrust in a globalised economy: The unique enforcement challenges faced by small and developing jurisdictions. *Fordham International Law Journal* 33(1): 1–56

Gerber D (2010) *Global competition: Law, markets and globalisation.* Oxford: Oxford University Press

Hausmann R, Hwang J & Rodrik D (2007) What You Export Matters. *Journal of Economic Growth,* 12(1): 1–25

Khan M (2006) Governance and Development. Paper presented at the Workshop on Governance and Development organised by the World Bank and DFID in Dhaka (11–12 November 2006)

Makhaya G, Mkwananzi W & Roberts S (2012) How should young institutions approach enforcement? Reflections on South Africa's experience. *South African Journal of International Affairs* 19(1): 43–64

North DC, Wallis JJ & Weingast B (2009) *Violence and social orders.* Cambridge: CUP

Page J (2012) Can Africa industrialise? *Journal of African Economies* 21(2): ii86–ii12

Rey P & Tirole J (2006) A primer on foreclosure. In M Armstrong & RH Porter (Eds) *Handbook of Industrial Organization III*. Amsterdam: North-Holland

Roberts S (2013) Competition policy, industrial policy and corporate conduct. In J Lin, J Stiglitz & E Patel (Eds) *The Industrial Revolution II: Africa in the 21st Century*. London: Palgrave

Rodrik D (2007) Normalizing industrial policy. Paper prepared for the Commission on Growth and Development. Cambridge, MA

Singh A (2004) *Multi-lateral competition policy and economic development*. UNCTAD Series on Issues in Competition Law and Policy, Geneva

Sutton J (2004) Competing in capabilities: Globalization and development. Clarendon Lectures in Economics, Department of Economics, University of Oxford

2 *Regional cartels and competition in the cement industry across six countries: Botswana, Kenya, Namibia, South Africa, Tanzania and Zambia*

Taimi Amunkete, Emmanuel Chokwe, Godfrey Gabriel, Michael Humavindu, Junior Khumalo, Thabiso Mbongwe, George Nguruse and Benson O Nyagol

Cement occupies a special place in competition policy discourse. Practitioners in a newly established competition authority attending international meetings with their counterparts will inevitably be asked when they are going to catch 'the cement cartel'. As competition expert Professor Richard Whish observed in 2001:

> 'The first thing for any new competition regulator is to go out and find the cement cartel. My experience of this subject is, it is always there, somewhere…The only countries in which I had been unable to find the cement cartel is where there is a national state-owned monopoly for cement.' (Majenge 2012: 1)

To understand why the cement industry is so inextricably linked with collusion, it is necessary to first look at the production process. Cement production is a typically large-scale industrial process, requiring the construction of a factory with substantial fixed costs. Key inputs also need to be sourced, including limestone or clinker made from limestone, and energy. Time and substantial capital investments are both crucial components for supply operations to begin. Cement is also bulky and expensive to transport.

The demand for cement comes from construction projects, ranging from large-scale infrastructure projects to housing. Demand is thus associated with infrastructure investment in the economy and is relatively insensitive to price. Cement itself is classified in different grades and needs to comply with standards to ensure that the structures made from it are secure. The products of different companies are essentially identical, however, as long as they comply with the relevant specifications.

These characteristics signify that typically a small number of long-established producers are to be found in any geographic market. Therefore, if companies agree on how to coordinate their activities, they can increase prices substantially while not suffering from significantly reduced sales. The only alternative for consumers may be to import cement from far afield, at high costs that could include any import tariffs that may be in place.

At the same time, there are strong short-term incentives for producers to discount sales to attract customers from their rivals. With established plants that are not operating at full capacity, producers can look to make an additional sale by undercutting the price of their rivals. In relation to suppliers to large construction projects, each supplier would like to get the business, so the buyer is in a good position to play the suppliers off against each other with the net prices being driven down. The implication is that competition can be vigorous, with keen pricing and substantial discounts to customers.

With a small number of producers and the difference in prices (and profit margins) between competition and coordination being so substantial, cement producers have a big interest in finding ways to restrain competition among themselves. Cement is thus a product that is prone to anticompetitive conduct, especially collusion (Hüschelrath et al. 2013). While there are other similar products, such as organic chemicals, where collusion has also been prevalent (see Connor & Helmers 2006), the ease with which people around the world can relate to cement – as a critical requirement for basic housing – has made it emblematic of collusion. The importance of cement in a country's economic development has also led to state involvement in the cement industry, including through direct ownership, the protection of local cement producers and legal cement cartels.

The major cement companies are also multinational operations: in southern and East Africa, the main firms are generally part of global corporations or have developed through associations with these groups. This has a number of implications. First, it is reasonable to expect that the practices they pursue in one region (such as collusion) will be replicated in others. Second, a country-by-country perspective is unlikely to reveal clearly the company strategies. For example, a company with operations in Kenya, Tanzania and Uganda would rationally be looking at optimising its business across East Africa as a whole.

In the six countries studied here, all these features have been present. From the 1940s until 1996, a legal cartel was effectively operating across the Southern African Customs Union (SACU) (comprising Botswana, Lesotho, Namibia, South Africa and Swaziland).[1] In a number of these countries, there has also been state ownership of cement companies, including in Kenya, where East African Portland Cement is still state owned. Botswana, Namibia, South Africa, Tanzania and Zambia are members of the Southern African Development Community (SADC), which has 15 member states. Kenya and Tanzania are members of the East African Community (EAC), which also includes Burundi, Rwanda and Uganda. Free trade of cement takes place between countries within these trade blocs.

In 2009, the South African Competition Commission uncovered and ended a cartel that had started to operate shortly after the ending of the legal arrangements in 1996, whereby the producers had coordinated their activities. Interestingly, the case revealed how the three producers – PPC, Lafarge and Holcim/AfriSam, (which jointly owned a fourth from the 1990s through to the mid-2000s) – had set up the cartel to avoid detection and to give the semblance of competition. The producers agreed on market shares across the whole of the SACU region and monitored the agreement through sharing monthly sales information. These arrangements were international in scope as they operated across Botswana, Lesotho, Namibia, South Africa and Swaziland as one area, notwithstanding the borders and substantial transport costs within and between some countries. The agreement also involved the allocation of a particular producer to certain countries to create more stability in the cartel and to make monitoring easier.[2]

The study was based on data collected up to and including 2012, with a comment on recent developments included in the review of observed outcomes later in this chapter.

The chapter is structured as follows: First, an overview of the production and distribution of cement is provided. Here after the structure of the cement industry and the extent of the operations of the main companies across the six countries covered in the study are reviewed. This is followed by the outcomes observed across the six countries, in particular the pricing of cement over time. The links between the observed outcomes and the competitively relevant features are then assessed, along with other pertinent factors such as trade protection and government regulations. The last section concludes.

Understanding the production and distribution of cement

Cement is a relatively low-value, high-weight product that is expensive to transport by land. It is therefore important to understand the geographic positioning of cement plants relative to the main sources of demand. Cement plants are generally located close to raw material inputs (such as limestone deposits) or close to ports, where key inputs can be imported. Logistical factors such as access to roads and railway lines are critical for accessing customers. This means that the most obvious markets for a producer may be across a national border.

Cement production uses well-established technology. It involves the quarrying and then crushing of primary raw material calcium carbonate or limestone. The crushed rock and other required ingredients are stored in stockpiles before blending takes place and a uniform quality of raw material is achieved. The main elements of cement are calcium oxide, silica, alumina and iron oxide. Once the blending process is completed, the meal is fed to homogenising silos, where it is carefully mixed to ensure that the kiln feed is uniform. The next stage involves the raw meal being burnt in the kiln to form cement clinker. The clinker is formed from the components of the raw meal reacting at high temperatures (900–1 500°C) in the precalciner and in the rotary kiln. As it is so important for the elements to be combined in the right proportions, systematic sampling and laboratory testing form an important part of the process. After cooling, the clinker is ground together with additives[3], and the resultant product is Ordinary Portland Cement (OPC). The additives can be used to 'extend' the product, to yield different strengths of the blended cement.

For efficient production, a good source of raw material input is required, together with a relatively large-scale production facility. The processes themselves are energy intensive, so the availability and cost of energy are important factors. Production plants in the six countries are typical, with some variations occurring mainly in the supply of raw material for cement production. The main raw materials used are limestone and fly ash, while the end raw material is clinker. Limestone is mined from quarries, while fly ash (a by-product of electricity generation) is often obtained either directly from electricity supply companies or indirectly through middlemen. Of the six countries, five (Namibia, Kenya, South Africa, Tanzania and Zambia) have large deposits of limestone, while there are only small deposits in Botswana.

A company entering the market requires substantial capital investment and access to critical inputs and needs to be able to distribute as well as manufacture the product (Figure 2.1), to be an effective competitor. A company can enter the market by first importing or buying clinker and engaging in the processes of grinding, blending and bagging. Importing or buying clinker is much less capital intensive, but it also means higher costs. With clinker comprising about 95% of the cost of inputs in cement manufacturing, it is normally important for companies to vertically integrate upstream, or to have long-term arrangements for securing inputs.

Figure 2.1 *The cement supply chain*

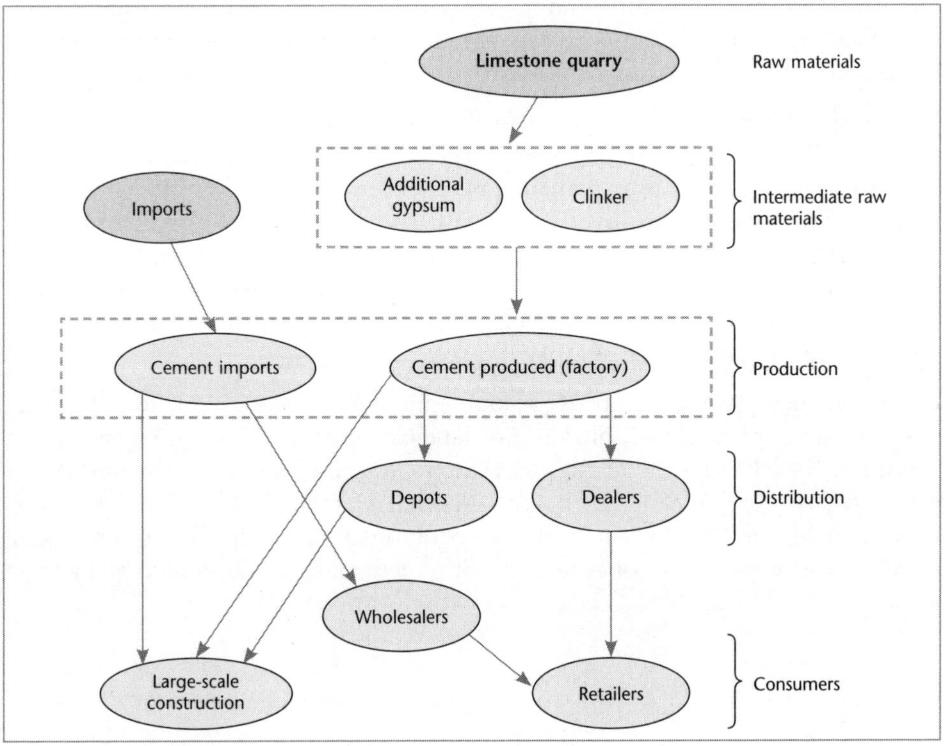

Source: Compiled by researchers

Most cement factories have clinker-producing capabilities through the processing of limestone, but in some instances factories are merely grinding facilities that source clinker from external suppliers with excess clinkering capacity, or they import clinker into the country. Cement producers in Namibia, Kenya, Zambia and South Africa also sell clinker. South African cement factories sell clinker to Botswana (which imports most – if not all – of its clinker), while in Tanzania all producers have grinding capacity that is larger than their clinker production capacity, which means that they sometimes import clinker from other countries. Across the six countries, cement producers usually have a physical presence in the countries in which they operate, but they also serve external export markets. There are also imports, either by independent trading companies or by large-scale consumers that import cement for their projects.

Cement is supplied in bulk to large customers and for major construction projects; it is generally distributed to smaller wholesale and retail customers in 50 kg bags.

The structure of the cement industry within and across the six countries

As already noted, the cement industry is a concentrated one, reflecting the importance of scale economies and the substantial capital investment required. This is especially true in relatively small economies, such as those of the countries covered in the study.

Historically, companies associated with three main groupings – Pretoria Portland Cement (PPC), Lafarge and Holcim/AfriSam – have dominated southern and East Africa (Figure 2.2), even while the nature of ownership and holding company arrangements have changed over time. South Africa has a fourth smaller producer Natal Portland Cement-Cimpor (NPC-Cimpor), which used to be jointly controlled by the other three, while Namibia had an entrant, Ohorongo Cement, in 2007. Botswana has a very small local producer of clinker, MPC, but is otherwise reliant on imported clinker and cement.

In Zambia, one producer, Lafarge, accounts for most of the production. Tanzania has three major producers – Tanzania Portland Cement (Heidelberg), Tanga Cement Company (Holcim) on the coast, and Mbeya Cement (Lafarge) in the west of the country close to the Zambian border. Maweni Cement (established by Kenya's Athi River Mining) started its Tanzania operations in 2012. In Kenya, the cement sector has also been very concentrated, with a few main producers led by Lafarge-associated Bamburi.

Figure 2.2 *Capacity by producer and country, in production in 2012*

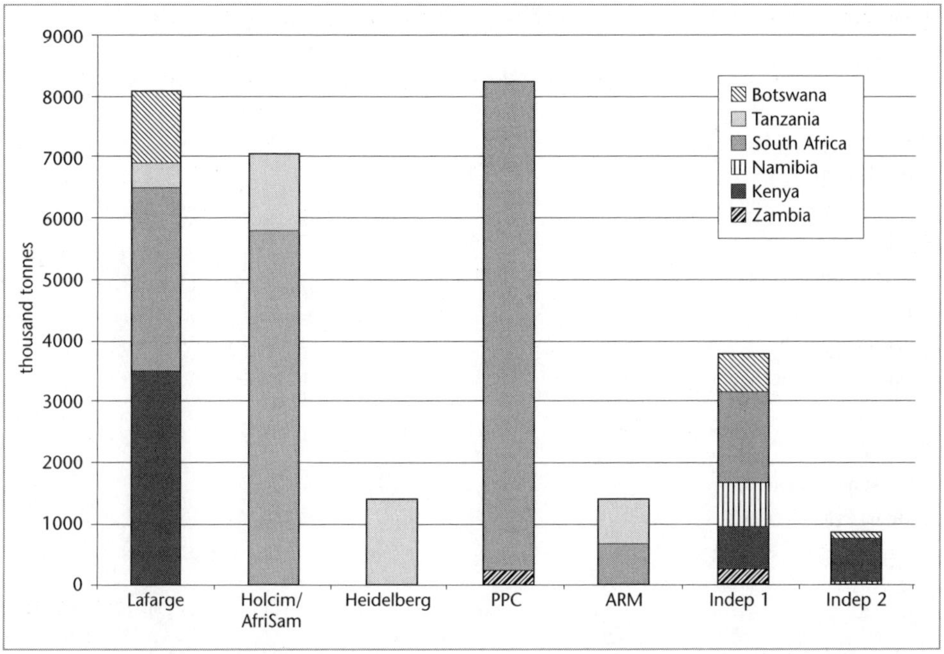

Source: Compiled by researchers (see Table 2.1), 2013

Note: Independent 1 and Independent 2 are different entities, as per Table 2.1, represented here separately by country.

While the study focused on the developments in the decade to 2012, there have been major changes in the form of new entrants, notably between 2013 and 2015. It is also interesting to note that with the industry having been dominated by firms with strong links to established players from Europe, along with South Africa's PPC, the newer entrants include firms from China and elsewhere in Africa. For example, Nigerian company Dangote Cement is investing in Tanzania, South Africa (in Sephaku Cement, which started production in 2014) and in Zambia (with production starting in 2015). Mombasa Cement, National Cement and Savannah Cement are all new entrants in Kenya. There are also a number of smaller producers, which are effectively downstream processing, blending and distribution operations of larger operations in neighbouring countries. The potential effects of these new entrants on competition are examined in the conclusion.

The new entrants clearly reflect the growing demand for cement arising from the prevailing high levels of infrastructure spending and rates of economic growth across the southern and eastern African regions. The entry of the new market players, along with the expansion of existing operations, suggests that attractive returns are expected.

Table 2.1 *Structure of the cement industry within and across the six countries, including new entrants*

Company and associated group	Country and production capacity (Actual and in pipeline) in tonnes per annum					
	Botswana	**Kenya**	**Namibia**	**South Africa**	**Tanzania**	**Zambia**
Athi River Mining (ARM)						
- ARM (Kenya)		650 000				
- Mkuranga/Maweni (Tanzania)					500 000	
Botsino	250 000					
Cemtech Sanghi Group*		1 200 000				
Dangote						
- Dangote (Tanzania)*					1 500 000	
- Sephaku Cement (South Africa)*				1 200 000		
- Dangote (Zambia)*						1 500 000
Holcim/AfriSam						
- AfriSam (Botswana)						
- AfriSam (South Africa)				5 800 000		
- Tanga Cement Co (Tanzania)					1 250 000	
PPC						
- PPC (Botswana)	225 000					
- PPC (South Africa)				8 000 000		
Jidong Cement*				1 000 000		
Lafarge						
- Bamburi (Kenya)		2 200 000				
- EAPCC (Kenya)		1 300 000				
- Lafarge (South Africa)				3 000 000		
- Lafarge (Botswana)						
- Lafarge (Zambia)						1 230 000
- Mbeya Cement (Tanzania)					350 000	
Lake Cement*					500 000	
Matsiloje Portland Cement (MPC)	35 000					
Mombasa Cement		700 000				
National Cement		700 000				
NPC-Cimpor				1 500 000		
Ohorongo			700 000			
Savannah Cement*		600 000				
Scirocco						109 500
Tanzania Portland Cement (Heidelberg)					1 400 000	
Zambezi Portland Cement						612 000

*Not yet producing cement, as of 2014

Source: Company annual reports, 2012

There are many factors affecting successful entry into the market, including the company's ability to access raw materials and obtain the necessary government approvals, as well as securing finance. These factors are discussed below. The crucial question is what effect these entrants have on competition and prices across the countries studied. The cross-country comparisons below provide an indication of what might be expected from more competitive markets and indications from pricing developments in 2014 and 2015 are that much more competitive outcomes have been realised in a number of countries, as noted in the concluding section.

The main cement producers in each country and where they operate

The cement markets in five of the six countries covered in the study, all have oligopolistic structures. The exception is Namibia, where there is a monopolistic structure. While Kenya appears to have a relatively large number of producers – eight if the new, planned entrants are included – some of them are very small and the impact that the new entrants will have is also unclear. This means that concentration in Kenya is still relatively high. While the joint share of the largest three firms was close to 100 per cent in 2012, this has subsequently declined.

Taking the six countries as a whole, Lafarge and PPC each account for 26% of the total capacity in 2012, followed by AfriSam with 22%, and then ARM, TPC (Heidelberg) and NPC – each with a 4% to 5% share in the total capacity. The South African cement producer PPC also has plants in Rwanda, Zimbabwe and Ethiopia (where it has a 27% share in Habesha). This is significant as these countries are neighbours to those covered in the study. Kenya's Bamburi Cement (Lafarge) has a substantial operation in Uganda (Hima cement) and in Zimbabwe. Interestingly, when the total capacity of each of the main producers across the six countries is compared, the capacity of companies associated with Lafarge, Holcim/AfriSam and PPC are quite close to each other, at around 7 million to 8 million tonnes (Figure 2.2).

The location of the plants is another important factor and the study examined this in relation to national borders. For example, while Mbeya Cement (Lafarge) is in Tanzania, it is actually just across the border from Zambia, in which Lafarge also dominates, and 850 kilometres from Dar es Salaam, the main market. There are two producers on the coast of Tanzania – Tanga Cement is 350 kilometres from Dar es Salaam, where TPC is located. In Kenya, ARM, Bamburi and East Africa Portland Cement Company (EAPCC) are close to Nairobi, while Mombasa Cement is 500 kilometres away in the port city of Mombasa, where ARM also has a second plant. In Zambia, all the plants are located around the capital Lusaka and the Copperbelt (in the main city of Ndola).

Ohorongo Cement is the sole cement producer in Namibia and began operations in December 2010. It is located close to Otavi in the north of the country. Before the establishment of Ohorongo Cement, the Namibian cement market was supplied by the South African cement producer AfriSam, which covered 95% of the Namibian market.

A very large proportion of cement demand in Namibia comes from the greater Windhoek, Walvis Bay and Swakopmund areas, as well as the northern parts of the country. These markets are all very far from what was the source of cement, AfriSam's Ulco cement plant situated near Kimberley in the Northern Cape Province of South Africa (for example, in the case of Windhoek, about 1 645 kilometres away).

Not all firms in the six countries are integrated directly into limestone mining operations. Factors to be considered include the prevalence of limestone deposits, the ability to get mining licences, the alternative option of importing, (which would involve factors such as proximity to a port and links to international sources of clinker), and the size of the demand to justify the scale of investment. For example, *Botswana* has limited limestone deposits, which are controlled by MPC in its Matsiloje Quarry. The other manufacturers therefore have to source fly ash and clinker material from neighbouring countries. The available limestone is in small quantities, which would not be enough for all the producers. Imports of clinker in Tanzania and Kenya have continued, despite there being available limestone deposits, which points to the need for investment to grow local production.

In *Kenya*, most of the cement manufacturers are vertically integrated. There are many limestone deposits and some limestone mining operations in different parts of the country, though more in the coastal region and the areas near Nairobi. Firms on the coast have clinker plants in the coastal region and have established grinding plants at Athi River, near Nairobi. Other companies, such as EAPCC and National Cement, have mining sites at Athi River, where they have established both clinker and cement plants. Most of the cement companies own the land on which they mine limestone and a few, such as National Cement, mine limestone on leased land. Imported clinker has also been used, and companies such as EAPCC are in the process of expanding their total clinker production to reduce costs on imported clinker. New entrants ideally should establish both a clinker and a clinker grinding plant at the point of entry, but this requires large amounts of capital.

In *Zambia*, the established producers are all vertically integrated. Lafarge Cement is directly integrated into limestone and shale mining operations at its quarries, and the rest of the raw materials are either acquired from other firms in the domestic market or imported from outside Zambia. For example, coal is produced locally at the Maamba Collieries and Collum Coal Mine in the Southern Province, gypsum from the Chambishi Mine in the Copperbelt Province, and sawdust from the Ndola city council in the Copperbelt Province. Bauxite is imported from Mozambique, and when there is a shortage of coal locally, it is imported from Hwange in Zimbabwe. Scirocco Cement and Zambezi Portland Cement are also vertically integrated into the input market. For example, Scirocco is the most integrated downstream into aggregates, block making and ready-mix concrete.

In *Namibia*, Ohorongo Cement is directly involved in the extraction of limestone near its production plant located near to Otavi in northern Namibia. These are far from the sources of local demand around Windhoek, Walvis Bay and Swakopmund. The alternative has been to import from South Africa.

Each cement producer in *Tanzania* that produces clinker has its own source of limestone, and facilities for producing and grinding clinker. Furthermore, one of the manufacturers uses its sister company for the distribution of cement and the other two operate their own distribution depots.

In *South Africa*, all the cement producers are vertically integrated, from the raw material inputs (such as limestone, fly ash and slagment) to cement, aggregates and ready-mix concrete. As limestone is an important input in the cement manufacturing process, it is important to have easy access to it and in sufficient volume. In spite of limestone being a scarce resource in South Africa, new entrant Sephaku Cement has managed to secure supplies by acquiring the mining rights from the mining firm Anglo American. Other limestone deposits are located far from the main markets.

There are also questions of downstream integration. Cement producers sell through various intermediaries such as wholesalers and retailers, as well as to ready-mix suppliers and to manufacturers of cast concrete products. The investigation into the South African cement cartel revealed that the practice of forward integration into ready-mix was common among the cement producers. By selling cement into each other's ready-mix concrete operations, the cement market could be divided. The investigation also uncovered the fact that the cement producers had planned to curtail the activities of cement-blending firms that buy clinker from them for further processing into cement. They planned to enter into vertical agreements to sell or grind clinker for each other as the primary cement producers.

Wholesalers are generally used for sales to smaller customers through retail outlets. For example, all three cement producers in Tanzania have used wholesalers to distribute their products. The wholesaler arrangement is such that costs of transport and the associated risks are solely the responsibility of the wholesalers/distributors.

The flow of trade

The trade flows in southern Africa reflect the fact that within the SACU, the South African cement producers viewed the five countries as one market. Botswana and Namibia therefore have recorded substantial imports. In Namibia, the product was mainly supplied by AfriSam as part of the cartel arrangements, while Botswana was largely supplied by PPC. Important changes have been the setting up of the Ohorongo plant in Namibia in 2007 and the supply by different producers into Botswana. In Namibia, Ohorongo Cement supplies the majority of the market. Therefore, while it appears that, at a country level, there is a monopoly in Namibia with a single producer, in fact this represents an increase in competition in the form of a new rival to the South African incumbents in the region. The effects on prices are examined in the next section.

South Africa has also exported to Mozambique, Angola, Zimbabwe, the Democratic Republic of the Congo (DRC) and Zambia. With regard to imports, South Africa has sourced cement mostly from Asia (mainly from the Republic of Korea, Pakistan, China, India and Indonesia) and the European Union (mainly France and United Kingdom); with some coming from Zimbabwe and Brazil (the only African and South American import sources, respectively). The imports were mainly driven by cement clinker, which contributed 41% of the imports, and are likely to have been sourced from related firms.

Trade flows in East Africa appear to be linked to production and location decisions by multinational producers, as well as deep-sea imports, which reflect an alternative to relying on local suppliers despite tariffs. In the case of Kenya, a net trade surplus on cement over the review period was maintained, with strong exports to the eastern African region. However, exports of cement to Uganda and Tanzania dropped after 2008, while exports to other countries increased. This appears to be linked to Kenyan cement firms establishing new plants in these countries, as well as expanding the capacity of the existing ones. For example, Bamburi doubled its capacity at the Hima plant in Uganda, while ARM established a subsidiary in Dar es Salaam.

Tanzania has consistently been a net importer from 2002, with Pakistan being its main source of cement imports. It is estimated that more than 80% of cement imports into Tanzania have been from Pakistan.[4] Tanzania exports cement mainly to countries in the region.

By comparison, Zambia has been a net exporter for all the years covered in the study, and substantially so since 2002. Imports are insignificant and are mainly at the border towns around the country. These imports come from some neighbouring countries and also from South Africa. Zambian producers export cement mainly to the DRC, the Great Lakes region and Malawi. Lafarge has reported mostly moderate exports of clinker to its sister company in Malawi. It is important to note that Zambian exports generally have been to countries that do not have a cement industry. This suggests that trade flows reflect the strategy of multinational companies not to compete with each other's subsidiaries.

It is clear that the trade flows, together with an understanding of the presence of firms across the region, support the need for the market dynamics of the region to be analysed more holistically.

Considering market outcomes

In this section, the market dynamics and pricing across the six countries are examined. (Prices are converted into US dollars as a common currency (Figure 2.3)). Then, moving to a country-by-country perspective, monthly pricing trends in local currencies are analysed.

Figure 2.3 *Estimated ex-factory cement prices, 50 kg bag, US$*

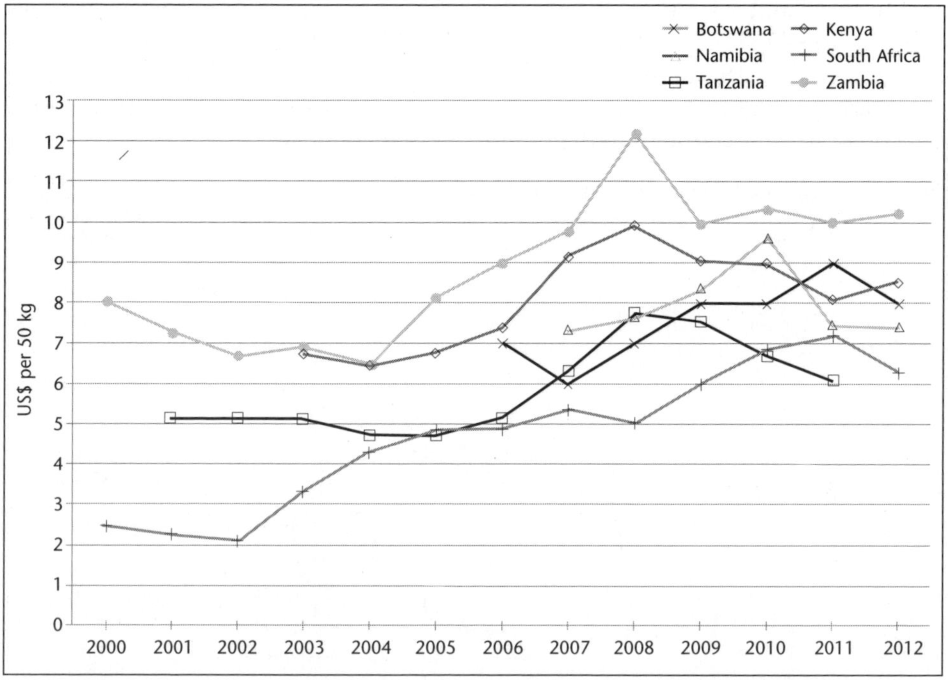

Sources: Averages were computed by researchers from data obtained from companies and national statistics.

Note: Kenyan and Tanzanian data was obtained from their respective National Bureau of Statistics (per tonne prices converted to per 50 kg and thus exclude bagging costs). South African data for 2008 to 2012 was extended to earlier years using the producer price index for ordinary and extended cement. Calculated in US$ using average annual exchange rates.

Market dynamics and pricing across the six countries

The estimated average annual ex-factory cement prices in US dollars for a 50 kg 32.5 MPa strength bag of cement in the six countries studied are compared for the period 2000 to 2012.

It is clear that throughout the period, Zambia's prices have remained above those of the other countries, accelerating between 2004 and 2008, before stabilising at around US$10 a bag between 2009 and 2012. Kenya has the second-highest prices for much of the period, although with something of a gap opening up in the last two years and with prices hovering at around US$8.50 in 2012.[5]

Prices in Tanzania appear to follow a similar trend to Kenya and Zambia, with which it shares important borders and transport corridors. However, the Tanzanian prices are substantially lower, especially in the most recent years for which data are available, with prices falling to US$6 in 2011. One of the reasons for lower prices in Tanzania is that deep-sea imports from sources such as Pakistan have set the ceiling to the pricing power of local producers. At times, local producers have lobbied government for protection, arguing that the increased imports harm the local industry.

In terms of retail prices, over the shorter period for which data has been compiled, it is clear that Zambia is the most expensive, apart from 2009 and 2010, when Namibia is higher (see Figure 2.4). It should be noted that in addition to retail margins being added, there are also transport costs to retail outlets around the countries where the prices are measured. This may explain why the retail prices in Namibia and Tanzania are higher by a greater margin than those in other countries.

Figure 2.4 *Estimated average retail cement prices, 50 kg bag, US$*

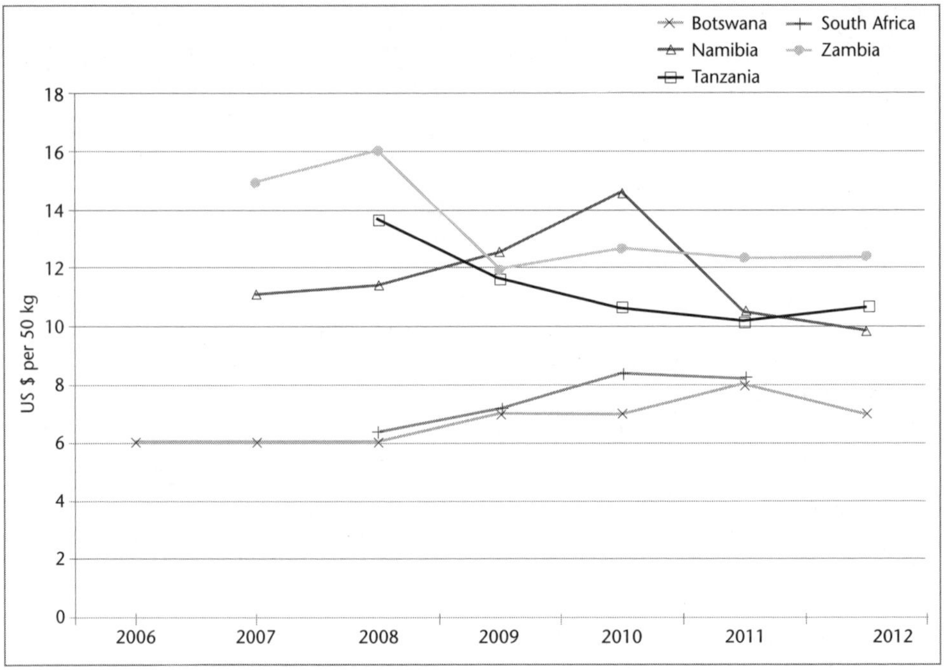

Sources: Surveys by authorities and researchers, including of large retailers in different countries, 2012 and 2013

Botswana, Namibia and South Africa: The cement cartel and after

In 2009, the South African Competition Commission uncovered a cement cartel that had been operating across the whole of the SACU since 1998. The operation of the cartel was integrally linked to the Cement and Concrete Institute (known as the C&CI), an industry association ostensibly responsible for advancing common industry concerns, and not for colluding.

At the heart of the cartel was an agreement on market shares across the SACU.[6] Each of the four producers, PPC, Lafarge, Holcim/AfriSam and NPC, provided monthly data on sales disaggregated by geographic regions within SACU, by product specification, by end-use sector (customer category), and also covering the imports of members. These data were then aggregated across the four producers by an audit firm appointed by the C&CI and this was fed back to the four producers. Each producer could then calculate on a monthly basis what its share was, across SACU, as well as track its share in different geographic regions and by different customer categories.

The South African Competition Commission put a stop to this information exchange (at least in its original form) in 2009, after having conditionally granted PPC immunity from being prosecuted. This followed a search and seizure operation conducted by the Commission on the cartel members in June 2009. The C&CI has since closed its doors.

The cement industry in South Africa had been run through a legal cartel dating back to the 1940s. Through various institutional arrangements, including the company known as Cement Distributors (South Africa) (Pty) Ltd (CDSA), sales and distribution were centralised and planned across two large regions of the country, the northern and southern region.[7] This involved fixing market shares, and balancing up actual deliveries against the stipulated market shares of the producers. Cement was priced on the basis of a model known as the Twycross pricing model, which optimised rail transport. This model used Lafarge's Lichtenburg plant as the base pricing point, from where all sales in the CDSA market area were priced, by adding the benchmark transport costs being used in the pricing model. Indeed, it was this very function that was notionally the *raison d'être* for the cartel: optimising the rail transport of cement to minimise the distribution cost of the product. This amounted to price fixing because it set a rule on delivered prices to customers.

The Competition Board of South Africa withdrew the exemption from competition law in 1995 and the companies were allowed until September 1996 to terminate the legal cartel arrangements. The period granted was to allow the companies time to establish their own sales, distribution, marketing and transport functions. Although the companies apparently agreed that they would maintain the same market shares as under the legal arrangement, this did not happen, and for around two years after the end of 1996 the producers competed among each other. In particular, PPC, which had the largest production capacity, sought to expand its market share, competing for customers on price and non-price terms.

In 1998, all the cement producers showed poor financial performance due to price competition, which led them to hold several preliminary meetings in Port Shepstone in KwaZulu-Natal to attempt to bring the market back to 'stability'. At these meetings, PPC was accused by Lafarge and AfriSam of breaching the market share agreement and spending too much money on promotions and the branding of its products, as well as discounting at a local and regional level. Among other things, these meetings resulted in agreement on pricing parameters for different types of cement, and cartel members agreed not to offer special discounts on higher quality cement.

It was also agreed that certain offices and depots would be closed in some regions. For example, it was agreed that PPC would not compete in northern Natal in exchange for Lafarge not competing with PPC in the Botswana market.[8] After the

Port Shepstone agreement, interactions with regard to the implementation of the arrangements continued until at least 2002.[9] It is also important to note that three of the producers – PPC, Lafarge and Holcim/AfriSam – had shared ownership of two companies (called Ash Resources and Slagment) with control over inputs of fly ash and slag (used as extenders), as well as of a smaller regional cement producer, NPC. The companies thus had several forums in place where they still met.

The impact of the cartel in the SACU appears evident in the sharp price increases between 2002 and 2005. This is also consistent with a strong increase in the margins of PPC as the largest producer – from 20% to 40% in 2005, measured as operating profits out of turnover (Figure 2.5). After the cartel was uncovered in 2009, it apparently took some time for competition to flow through to pricing, as local currency prices only fell in late 2010 (Figure 2.6).

Figure 2.5 *PPC operating profit margins, as percentage of turnover*

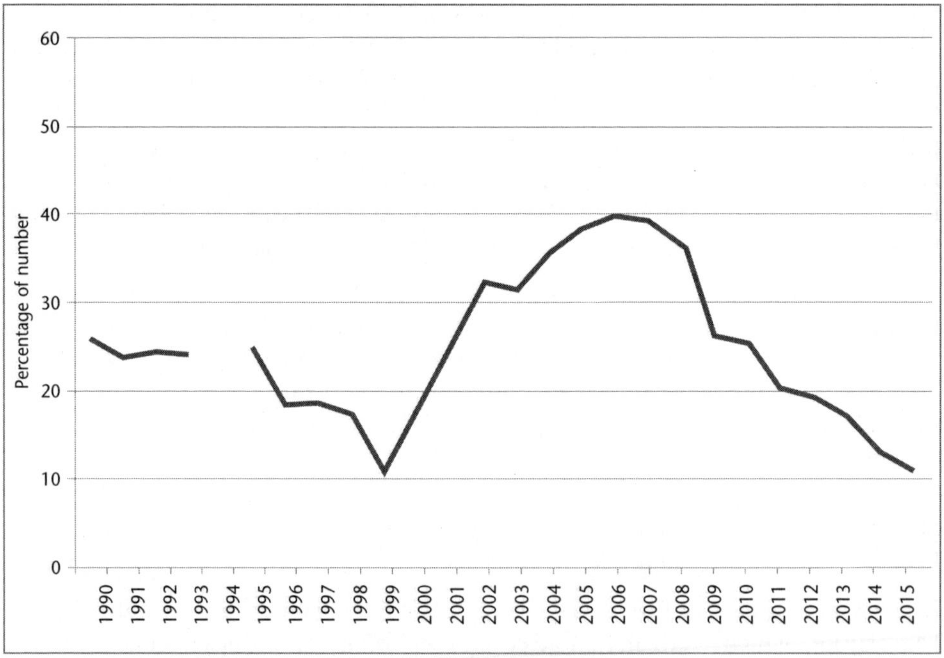

Source: Authors' calculation based on data from various annual financial reports, 2015

The Botswana prices track the South African prices, being marked up above these prices. This is consistent with higher transport costs and the fact that the cartel effectively allocated the Botswana market to PPC.[10] By comparison, the Namibia prices fell sharply in US dollar terms in 2011, consistent with the start of operations by the new entrant Ohorongo in December 2010. Based on a comparison with South African prices (a mark-up from 2007 to 2010 of around \$2 to \$2.50), the new entrant brought benefits of lower prices with a drop of about \$2 (or around 25%), measured on an ex-factory basis.

Figure 2.6 *South African producer price index for ordinary and extended cement*

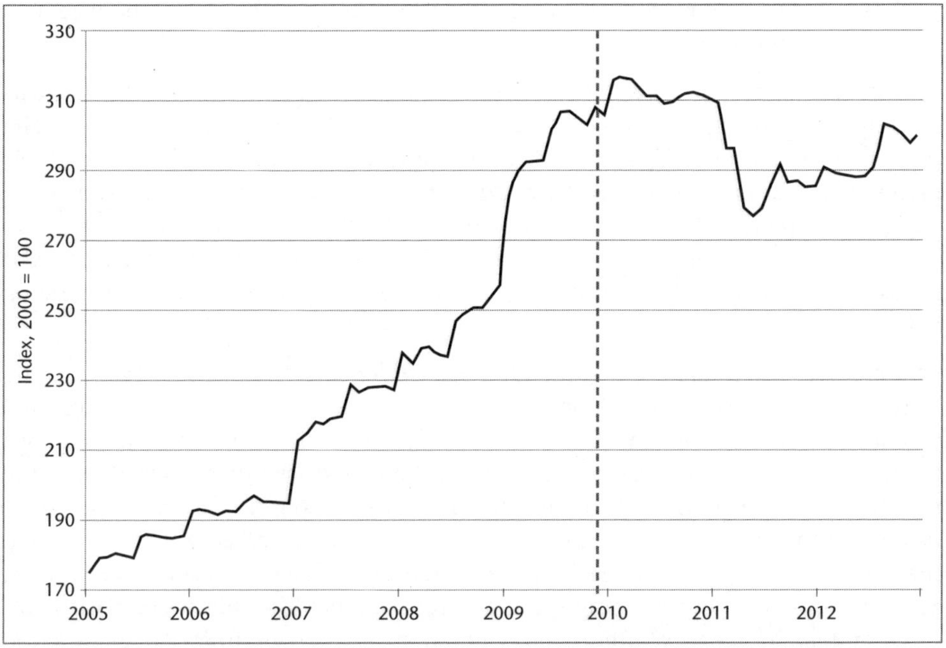

Source: Statistics South Africa, 2013

Note: The dashed line denotes the leniency agreement of PPC and its announcement, meaning the end of the cartel.

The nodal pricing system and information exchange

Under the cartel, price monitoring also seems to have been supported by a nodal pricing strategy adopted by PPC, Lafarge and others from 2001 onwards. The nodal pricing system meant that PPC committed to not discounting on prices (outside of fixed discounts on price lists), and that customers within a node were charged the same price. Prices were determined at executive level for 'nodes', which were geographic regions or zones of supply. Therefore towns in any given node would pay the same price irrespective of their distance from the core. Different nodal prices were calculated for different cement products and packaging options. As these were transparent to other producers, it allowed them to follow PPC's pricing.

The critical point about the arrangements is the role of information exchange on supply volumes and the understanding about market shares in ensuring that prices were adhered to. The incentive to discount (or 'cheat' on the arrangement) existed because of the attraction of winning a larger share of the juicy profits, even with the slightly lower margin that would result from the secret discounting. The availability of sales information meant that each firm could see if such a strategy was being followed by a rival, and where and in what customer segment the discounting to win over customers was taking place. This, in turn, meant that the other firms could retaliate and that the increase in share would thus be short-lived and the incentive to cheat greatly reduced.

The impact in terms of maintaining closely matched price increases, and firms sticking to the price, is evident in the producer price index data (Figure 2.6). The price increases are readily observable, indicating that the firms all increased their prices at the same time. The leniency agreement reached with PPC and the South African Competition Commission (and the exit of PPC from the cartel arrangement) in August 2009 and the Commission's press release in November 2009, which served notice on the other cartel members, was then followed by changes in the pricing pattern.

The markets in Namibia and Botswana are evidence of the cartel largely having allocated each country to one supplier, and of neither country having local integrated production capacity of any significance at the time. The information exchange maintained this effective market division. In the case of Namibia, AfriSam was the supplier, while Botswana was supplied by PPC. In each country the end of the cartel has meant the entry of other suppliers. Larfarge, in particular, actively has supplied into each country in recent years and there appears to have been some variation in pricing. However, there is an important difference in that Namibia has seen the entry of Ohorongo. The start of Ohorongo's operations saw a substantial price reduction in 2011 in nominal local currency terms (Figure 2.7), as well as relative to other countries as indicated in Figure 2.3 on page 19.

Figure 2.7 *Namibian average annual ex-factory gate prices (N$, per 50 kg bag)*

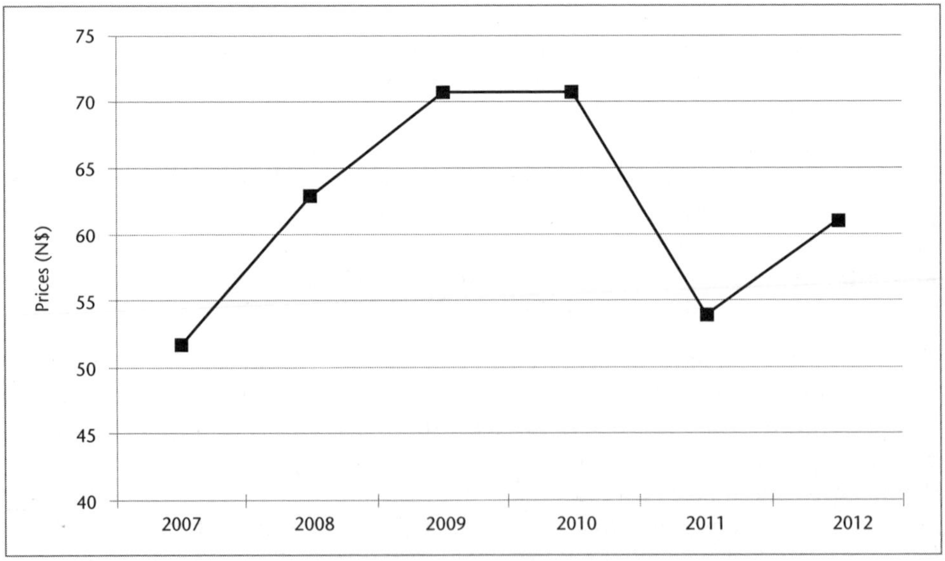

Source: Major retailer/Ohorongo Cement, 2013

While Botswana did not experience such a price reduction, the end of the cartel brought more meaningful competition from other suppliers. Data from a major South African-based building materials retailer that has branches in other southern African countries, including Botswana and Namibia, show that PPC had the highest prices. As indicated, while AfriSam may have registered lower prices in some stores (possibly on the Namibia border) it did not offer volumes, so that PPC effectively set the price. However, in 2009 and 2010, PPC's prices dropped to meet those of AfriSam, indicating effective competition from AfriSam's supply into the country (Figure 2.8). In addition, Lafarge entered Botswana in December 2009, with lower prices.

Figure 2.8 *Prices to major retailers in Botswana for bagged cement (3 month moving average)*

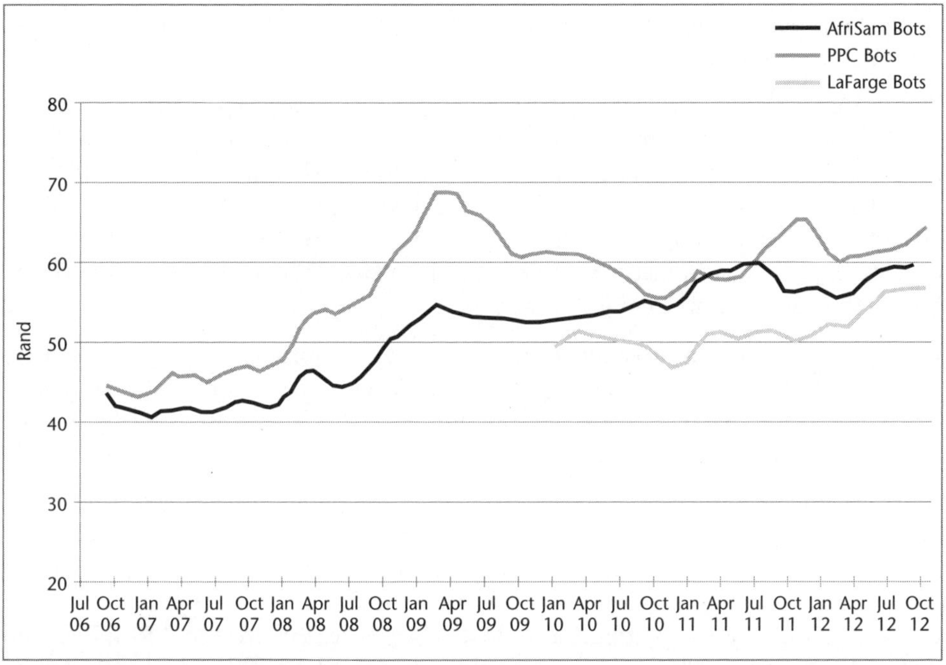

Source: Various retail stores in Botswana, 2013

Information on profit margins for PPC, the only producer publicly listed, is consistent with the impact of the cartel. Margins measured simply by operating profit as a percentage of revenue reveal a declining trend from 1995 to 1999, after which a strong recovery is witnessed until 2006 (Figure 2.5). At this point, the margins are in excess of 40 per cent. The decline between 1995 and 1999 coincides with the period of price wars in the South African cement industry following the termination of the legal cartel in 1996. The recovery from 1999 also coincides with the subsequent illegal cartel agreement between cement producers in 1998. A further sharp decline is seen from 2009 to 2011, where the margin reached 27%. The available data also reveals that margins from the South African cement operations are in line with the overall margin, reflecting the dominance of the South African business in the total. Margins from other African operations, however, show a contrasting trend. These operations were very small over the period studied and included the PPC plant in Zimbabwe. Sales into Botswana were essentially made from South Africa, meaning that the transfer price would influence the margin made.

Kenya, Tanzania and Zambia

Kenya and Tanzania both have had tight oligopolies with two to three major producers. They also overlap in that Lafarge and more recently Athi River Mining (ARM) have been operating in each country. Tanzania has Tanzania Portland Cement (Heidelberg) and Tanga Cement, which both have more than 1 million tonnes of capacity, while Kenya also has Mombasa Cement, National Cement and Savannah Cement, each somewhat smaller.

Kenya and Tanzania are both members of the EAC, which identified cement as a sensitive product and imposed a 55 per cent external tariff. This has been reduced in several steps from 2010, but, while in force at this level, it meant that competition within the EAC was even more important in determining prices, as the external tariff effectively increased the limit to the exertion of market power provided by deep-sea cement imports. An industry organisation also exists that covers the whole of the EAC – the East African Cement Producers Association.

Comparisons of prices between the countries at the producer level (ex-factory) indicate that Kenyan prices have been substantially higher than Tanzanian prices. There are a number of possible reasons for this, which are discussed before the situation in Zambia is addressed.

In *Kenya*, there have been, and remain, cross-shareholdings between the major producers. Lafarge's Bamburi business, the largest producer in the region with 2.2 million tonnes of capacity, continues to have cross-shareholdings with the EAPCC in which the government of Kenya – through different entities – holds the controlling interest. Bamburi also held a 14 per cent interest in ARM, but then divested from it in 2009.[11] Cross-shareholdings such as these are widely recognised as having a dampening effect on competition. They assist in creating the climate for a common understanding to be reached (including through directors) and can mean a presumption of an agreement in some jurisdictions.[12] Even passive shareholdings change the incentives to set prices, as some of the earnings from sales diverted to a rival are now internalised.

Another difference between Kenya and Tanzania is that Kenya had a national tariff of 40%, reduced to 25% in 2008. Kenya prices at the ex-factory level continued to increase in local currency terms, with substantial increases of around 40 per cent from 2006 to 2008 (see Figure 2.9).

Figure 2.9 *Kenya cement prices (Kenyan Shillings (KES) per tonne)*

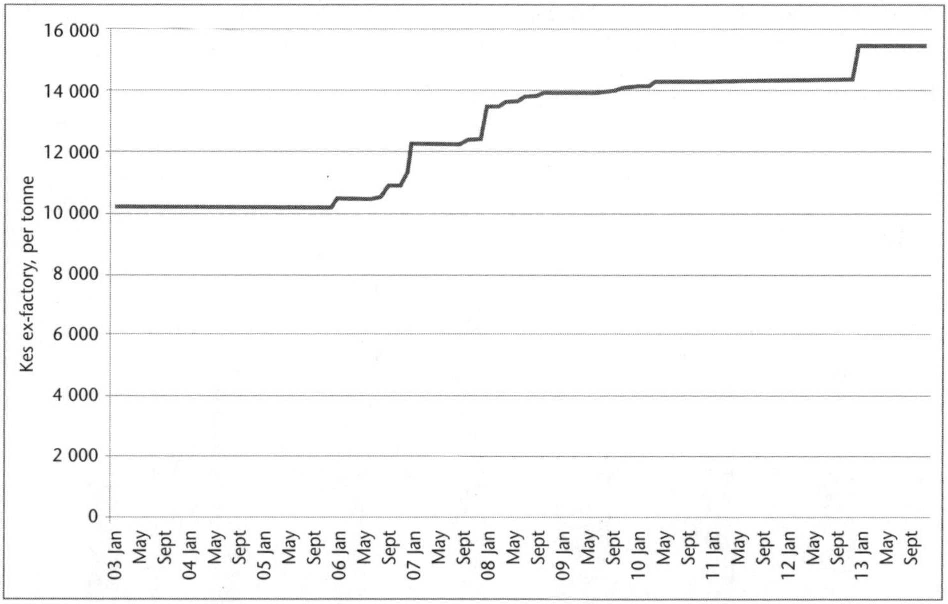

Source: Kenya National Bureau of Statistics, 2013

Kenya has seen new entry, but it is not clear whether this has made a difference. The entrants include Mombasa Cement, which entered in 2009, and National Cement, which commissioned its plant in June 2011.[13] Mombasa Cement has the backing of the Taiheiyo Cement Corporation, the largest cement producer in Japan, while National Cement is associated with the Kenyan Devki Steel business. Both are committed to expanding output and are integrated back into clinker. While newspaper reports have suggested lower prices being offered by the entrants,[14] the official statistics indicate only that nominal price increases were negligible from mid-2008 through to late 2012. After 2012, it appears that the new entrants did have an impact on prices.[15]

A comparison with South African prices also points to somewhat improved outcomes. Ex-factory prices in Kenya were more than 50 per cent higher than the South African prices from 2003 to 2009 (and note that the South African prices were already those pertinent under an admitted cartel). Between 2010 and 2012, the difference was reduced, with Kenyan prices being around 25 per cent higher than the South African prices. This period also coincided with the end of the southern African cartel – indicating that the South African prices were being set competitively.

The operating margins of listed companies provide some support for the notion that more competitive outcomes have been realised from 2010 onwards. The largest producer, Bamburi, has continued to record strong margins, but these have been reducing from the peak in 2009 (Figure 2.10). EAPCC's margins have been consistently lower than other firms, but it has relied on imported clinker and has been widely reported to have old equipment and low efficiency levels.

Figure 2.10 *Operating profit margins, as percentage of sales revenue – Kenya*

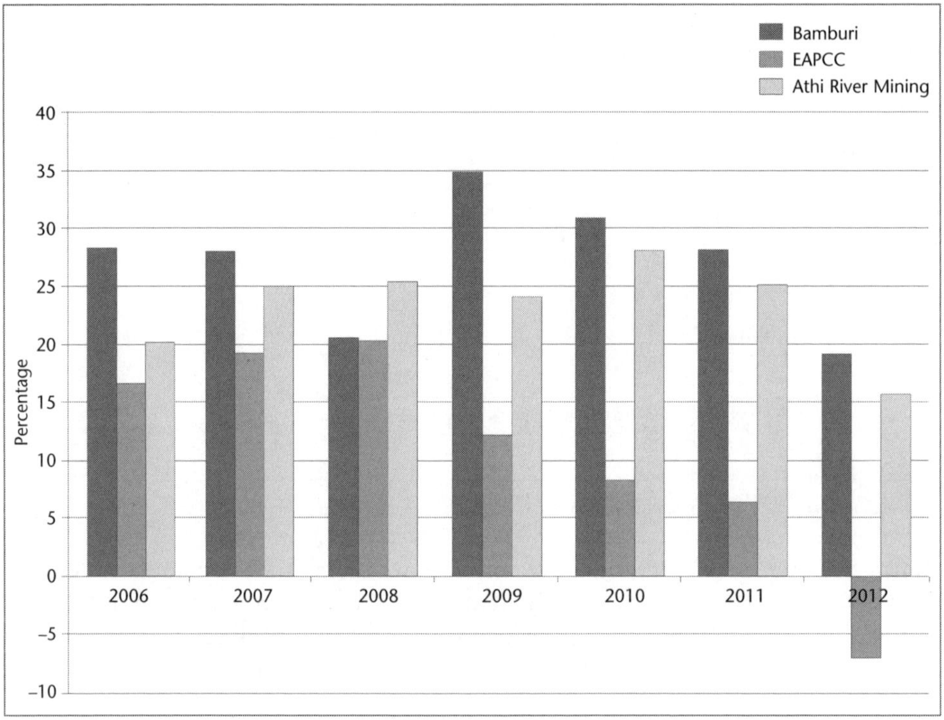

Source: Published financial results of companies, 2013

In *Tanzania*, in 2007, the cement price increased significantly, by more than 30% in both local currency and in US dollar terms (Figure 2.3 on page 19, and Figure 2.11). The government of Tanzania initiated two interventions to curb the soaring cement prices. The first measure was undertaken in 2007, whereby importation within the EAC was allowed at zero tariff. The intervention did not work as the prices remained at peak, which points to the apparent weak competition within the region. The second measure was undertaken in 2008, whereby the government allowed the importation of cement from outside the EAC by removing the suspended duty. This led to reductions in both the ex-factory price and the dealers' price (Figure 2.11). As reflected in Figure 2.3 on page 19, in US dollar terms, the Tanzanian price in 2011 was the lowest of all the countries being studied.

Figure 2.11 *Cement prices in Tanzania before and after government interventions*

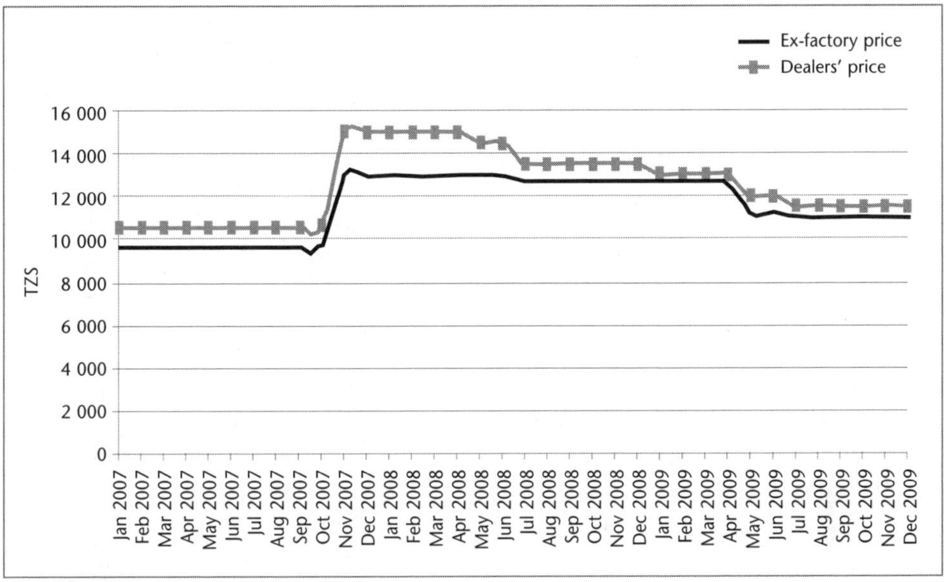

Source: FCC, 2010

The manufacturers claimed that the 2007 hike in prices was a result of profiteering by unscrupulous traders, coupled with a supply–demand mismatch, due to internal production capacity constraints. There are also questions about the pricing to different distributors, depending on the distance of the market from factory. Manufacturers priced on a delivered basis to distributors such that there were, in effect, higher ex-factory prices to those closer to the factory.

In *Zambia*, the market structure was characterised by a monopoly producer from 1949 to 2005, namely Lafarge Zambia. In 2005, Scirocco Enterprises Ltd entered the market and the price of the dominant player dropped slightly the following year (Figure 2.12), even though the competition offered by Scirocco Enterprises was insignificant, owing to its limited production capacity. In 2009, Zambezi Portland Cement entered the market and the prices dropped slightly in the following year, although the upward trend continued thereafter. International comparisons show that Zambian ex-factory prices were substantially higher than in other countries over the period, and at times close to double those in South Africa, the lowest priced country.

Figure 2.12 *Zambian ex-factory price trend for the three players in the sector (Kwacha)*

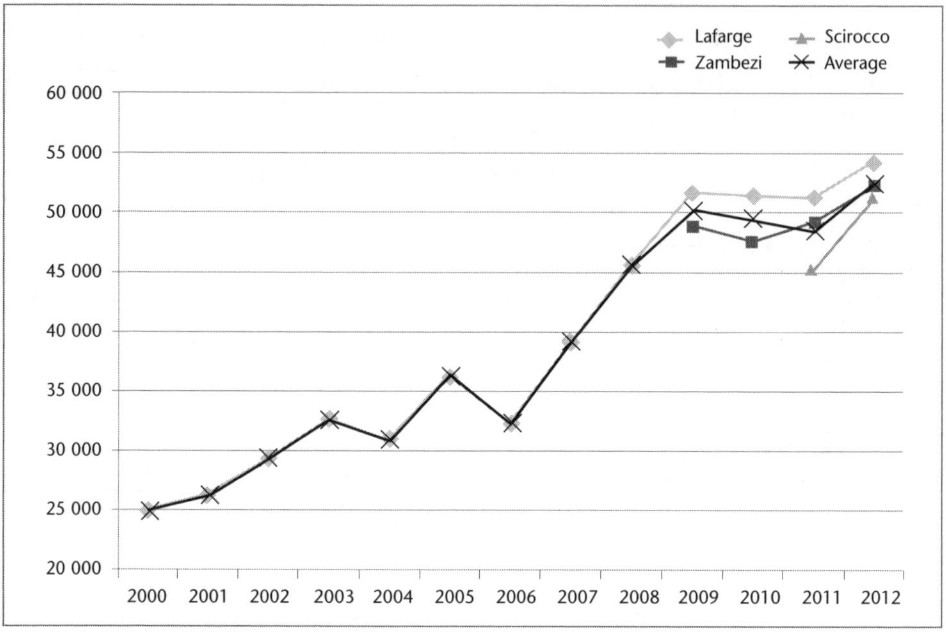

Source: Competition and Consumer Protection Commission of Zambia, 2013

The entry of the two small cement firms in the market did not appear to offer significant or effective price competition against Lafarge Cement. This is unsurprising as the companies are small and Lafarge continued to have substantially more than 60% of the local capacity, until the entry of Dangote Cement in 2015. Zambia has also sustained high prices while being a substantial net exporter. This suggests that increased volumes could be directed to the local market, but instead were being sold into export markets, possibly at lower returns given the transport costs involved. Margins of the main producer Lafarge have been strong (Figure 2.13). Examining average revenue from local and export markets suggests that the prices are similar.[16] However, distribution expenses are recorded separately, which indicates that if exports on average involve greater transport costs then the net prices are lower on an ex-factory basis.

In addition, despite having excess capacity and apparently very healthy margins, Lafarge Zambia has historically only exported to the DRC, Burundi and, mainly in later years, Malawi (where it has a sister company). In other words, exports have only been sent to countries that do not have local, established cement producers. There have been no exports to neighbouring countries such as Tanzania, Botswana, Namibia and Zimbabwe, where companies associated with Lafarge, PPC and Holcim/AfriSam have operated.

Figure 2.13 *Lafarge Zambia, operating profit margins, as percentage of turnover*

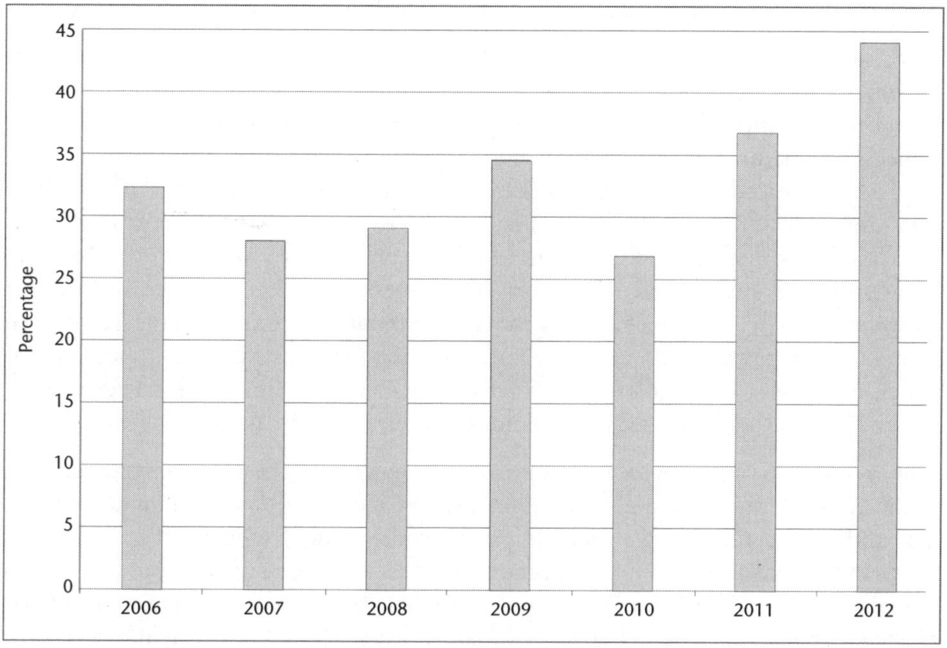

Source: Lafarge Cement Zambia annual reports, 2013

Understanding the outcomes observed

This assessment of market dynamics and outcomes points to the importance of understanding the behaviour of the firms in the market and whether they are competing, coordinating or if there is unilateral pricing power. This section considers issues of barriers to entry, competition concerns and the role of regulations and industry associations. Industry associations may play an important role, as illustrated in the SACU cartel above. The positive impact of new entrants in bringing increased competition into a market is also highlighted, as well as how regulations may raise barriers to such entry. In addition, trade protection means that competition that could be operating across borders is restricted, with substantial potential negative consequences for users of cement.

Barriers to entry

In order to understand the barriers with regard to entry to an industry, it is important to identify the factors that make it possible for a firm not only to enter a particular market but also to be able to grow to the point of posing a material threat to the existing players. There is also a distinction between barriers that arise due to the intrinsic nature of the products and activities in question (and which can be viewed as exogenous to the decisions of existing firms), and those associated with the incumbent firm's conduct, which may result from strategic decisions by the incumbent firms.

It is clear that across the countries covered in the study, the capital-intensive nature of cement and the scale economies relative to the size of local demand have been a deterrent to entry. On average, the capacity of a minimum efficient 'world-scale' cement-producing plant is approximately 2.5 million tonnes per annum, with start-up costs estimated in 2013 at approximately R3 billion or US$300 million. Scale economies are more significant in small markets such as Namibia and Botswana. Securing limestone, as a critical input to clinker production, further means locating an appropriate source and negotiating the necessary rights and permissions for its mining.[17] This also depends on the government stance to new investment. In Namibia, the government is enthusiastic and open to investment opportunities, which minimises the regulatory obstacles. The source of limestone however, may, not be close to the main area of demand. Botswana has similar challenges.

The inland Gauteng Province in South Africa has the highest demand for cement in the country and there are no accessible limestone reserves for potential entrants. It is understood that to be a credible player in the cement industry it is crucial for the firm to have access to its own limestone reserves. There are limestone reserves available in the North West Province next to Gauteng, where Sephaku Cement has erected a plant. It took Sephaku approximately two years to secure the mining rights, as well as water and environmental licences, adding to the time required to enter the market. The decision to enter the market was taken in 2007 and cement production began in February 2015.

The decision to enter the market was influenced by Sephaku Cement's acquisition of limestone reserves from Anglo American in 2006 as a consequence of the South African government's use-it-or-lose-it principle in relation to minerals. Sephaku Cement then secured its first limestone mining right in February 2009.[18] Production of clinker is at Aganang, near Lichtenburg in the North West Province, with a capacity of 2.5 million tonnes per annum. This clinker is processed into cement at both Aganang and at a plant in Delmas, in Mpumalanga, using extenders secured by Sephaku Cement through a long-term agreement with Eskom for fly ash. At the very least then, it took eight years between Sephaku Cement's acquisition of limestone reserves and its first cement output. This long period can be attributed to a number of factors, including regulation and the securing of investors. The design and construction of the plants began at the end of 2010 and took approximately three years.

In Botswana, the main barriers to entry and expansion are those of availability and access to main inputs, which are fly ash and clinker material. With new entrants mostly beginning their cement production process at the grinding and blending stages, they currently find that their costs are high, due to the need for importing clinker, which is more expensive than those locally produced.

In addition to the capital investment required and securing sources of key inputs, other barriers that have been highlighted in Zambia include the high cost of freight and weak infrastructure, such as the poor condition of roads and railways, and erratic power supply. The existence of these barriers to entry into the cement sector in Zambia has, however, not stopped firms from entering the market, although the entrants to date are small. This changed in 2015, when the major investment being made by Dangote came on-stream. As with Dangote's Sephaku investment, this has taken a long time to plan and bring to fruition, with extensive regulatory hurdles that had to be overcome. The construction of the US$400 million plant started in July 2011.

Dangote has also constructed a cement plant in the south of Tanzania, at Mtwara, where there have been large discoveries of natural gas. This expansion can be compared with the expansion of PPC beyond its traditional markets in the SACU and Zimbabwe. PPC has focused more on acquisitions, including plants in Rwanda and Ethiopia, along with investments in new facilities across southern and East Africa.

In Tanzania and Kenya, the access to deep-sea cement imports has seen incumbents lobbying for protection through the East African Cement Producers Association (EACPA). The joint effort through the EACPA was, and is still, to see cement reinstated after it lost its 'sensitive status' at the EAC level in 2008. Kenya has imposed national duties, while Tanzania has not. After the introduction of imports in Tanzania, there have been allegations that imports are subsidised and substandard, and that duties are not paid properly. According to the Tanzania Bureau of Standards, all cement imports are subject to standard verifications and as far as the bureau is concerned, all imports in the market have passed the required standards, otherwise they would not be allowed in. The general public opinion is that since the introduction of imports, domestic manufacturers have found it difficult to raise prices, compared to the period before. As noted above, entrants in the Kenyan market appear to have had an impact on prices in 2013 and 2014, bringing into question the previous intensity of competition among the incumbents.

Competition law concerns by country and region

The Southern African Customs Union and the cartel

The most significant competition-related issue over the period has been the uncovering of the cartel across the SACU region. A number of lessons can be drawn from the operation of the cartel. First, at the heart of the arrangements was market division and information exchange through the industry association. This effectively removed price competition, as the commitment by the major producer to a pricing structure meant other producers could readily align their prices to it, while the market sharing meant there was no incentive to discount.

Second, the arrangements worked across countries for the SACU as a whole, in terms of fixing the overall market shares of each supplier at this level. This meant that if any country was analysed individually, the stability in market shares was not as clear, and in some countries (such as Lesotho, Swaziland and Namibia) the cartel arrangements appeared rather as unilateral market power, as there was effectively only one supplier.

Third, the cement firms had a history of vertical and horizontal relationships, which reinforced their position. These included jointly tying up critical supplies of extender materials such as fly ash and slag, while also having joint shareholding in the smaller regional producer, NPC-Cimpor. With the advent of the Competition Act in South Africa in 1998, the companies had actually made changes to several of these arrangements, such as divesting from NPC in around 2004, and changing the ownership of the inputs supply companies to one company, with supply agreements with the others.

Fourth, the companies were well aware of risks related to competition legislation and regulations, having previously had an exemption, which allowed the legal cartel to continue until 1996 when the exemption was ended by the then Competition Board of South Africa. The industry was also subject to the first (and unsuccessful) search and seizure operation of the newly formed Competition Commission in August 2000. Several of the producers (Lafarge, Heidelberg and Holcim) in the region have been found guilty several times of cartel conduct in other jurisdictions, over decades.[19]

In Botswana, MPC has access to the available and limited limestone in Matsiloje Quarry, while other manufacturers have to source fly ash and clinker material from neighbouring countries. The available limestone is in small quantities, which would not be enough for all the producers. Currently the available fly ash in the Morupule Colliery Mine is given on a contractual basis, making it difficult for other cement players to source it. The agreement in place only allows PPC Cement to source the available fly ash. With PPC Botswana being vertically integrated with the South African plant, it makes it easier to source its input materials, unlike other players, who are forced to find alternative sources for their inputs. This therefore requires high capital investment into key inputs from new entrants, as they may need to set up a clinker and cement plant, which could create a barrier to entry and possibly also to expansion.

In Namibia in 2010, a proposal was submitted for a merger between AfriSam and Ohorongo Cement. The merger proposed that Ohorongo Cement and AfriSam Namibia enter into an agreement under which AfriSam would sell and distribute cement under the management and brand of Ohorongo Cement in Namibia and neighbouring countries. The proposed merger was prohibited on the grounds that the supply agreement would potentially lead to the prevention or lessening of competition, or the restriction of trade or the provision of any service, or endangering the continuity of supplies in the cement market as provided for under Section 47(2)(a) of the Competition Act of 2003. Ohorongo Cement then independently started production in early 2011 and soon after, AfriSam closed its operations in Namibia, citing the inability to compete with locally produced cement as its reason for closure.

The East African Community and Zambia

Arrangements in the EAC and the operations of the EACPA point to similar competition concerns as those arising in the SACU. Companies appear to export into certain countries and not others.

While Zambia is not in the EAC or SACU, it is significant that it has exported to Burundi and the DRC and not to other countries, and that there have not been imports from neighbouring countries, such as Zimbabwe (where the main two producers are Lafarge and PPC). What appears to be unilateral pricing power when considered simply in terms of Zambia may appear to be the result of coordination, or at least oligopoly interaction across borders, when one considers it from a regional perspective across countries. The competition dynamics in terms of investment decisions that shape the competitive landscape must also be understood over time. The existence of significant scale economies makes competition across the region even more important. The closest plant for some consumers in a country may be across a national border (as with the east of Zambia, being close to Mbeya in Tanzania). However, the plant in Mbeya is owned by Lafarge and is unlikely to compete with the Lafarge operations in Ndola and Lusaka.

In terms of market share, Lafarge has dominated the cement industry in Zambia, followed by Zambezi Portland Cement and Scirocco. The industry has clearly been highly concentrated with limited competition. The dominant player,[20] Lafarge, has influenced market conditions in the industry and especially in terms of pricing strategy. The smaller firms, Zambezi Portland Cement and Scirocco, have to a large extent apparently followed the market leader in its pricing strategy, instead of offering competition – as is evident in the minor differences in their ex-factory prices. As a result of ineffective competition in the domestic market, prices have been very high. The lack of import competition for cement in the domestic market has exacerbated the price levels. At the time of the study, there were insignificant levels of imports coming into the country, and these were concentrated mainly in the border towns of the country. While Zambia is a net exporter of cement to countries in the region, including the DRC and the Great Lakes region, where prices may be higher, there are also neighbouring countries with lower prices, such as Tanzania.

In Kenya, one firm, Lafarge (and the business it controls, Bamburi Cement), has had shareholdings across all three of the producers. While it subsequently divested from one of them (ARM), it retains a substantial stake in the other, EAPCC. The fact that Lafarge has a stake in EAPCC, which allows it to appoint two board members, is a concern as this gives the firm access to its strategy, which may reduce competition. The local market has also been protected by tariffs, despite Kenya being a net exporter and having good resources for cement manufacture.

In Tanzania, the cement market has effectively been divided into three parts, according to geographical location of producers (in Tanga, Mbeya and Dar es Salaam). However, the Dar es Salaam market has been shared by all producers and importers. A comparison of prices in Dar es Salaam found that they were lower than the prices in the other local markets, which suggests limited competition in these markets. These distributors then sell to retailers, block layers and other end users. Distributors have limited influence on the prevailing market price as they are usually given an indicative price by the manufacturer.

The regulatory environment and industry associations

The role of government

Governments play a significant role in the cement industries of the six countries covered in the study, but to varying degrees. For example, in some countries (such as Tanzania), the government has been designated cement as a strategic commodity with investors receiving preferential treatment and being guaranteed zero-rated import duty and VAT deferment on project capital goods, favourable investment capital allowances and deductions, recognition of private property and protection against any non-commercial risks. Investors have also been guaranteed that they can repatriate all profits, gains and dividends from investment after tax.[21]

In all six countries, there are significant regulatory hurdles to setting up a cement factory, some of which go beyond requirements such as environmental impact assessments, rezoning of the land to be used, and complying with labour legislation. For example, securing a mining licence for the mining of limestone can be a significant hold-up. In another case, it took a new entrant 18 months to comply just with immigration legislation. These regulatory requirements are considered much more daunting by entrants than, for example, securing finance for constructing the cement factory, as they may take years and large amounts of money before the first brick to build the factory is laid.

Trade restrictions

Regional trade blocs have opened up trade between countries. The countries studied here straddle the SACU, the SADC and the EAC. Botswana, Namibia and South Africa (together with Lesotho and Swaziland) are members of the SACU, meaning that these countries can freely trade in cement with each other. There are, however, exceptions, such as Article 26 of the SACU Agreement of 2002, which gives certain industries infant industry protection for a period of about eight years. In Namibia, however, the intention of granting infant industry protection in 2012, with an import duty of 60% to be imposed until 2014 reducing thereafter, was blocked by court challenges from the Namibian importers of cement.

Together with Botswana, Namibia and South Africa, Tanzania and Zambia are members of the SADC, which has 15 member states in total. Again, this should mean free trade of cement between these countries, although the SADC agreements on trade have not been implemented by all countries.

Kenya and Tanzania are members of the EAC, which also includes Burundi, Rwanda and Uganda. Under an agreed EAC Protocol, cement was for a period considered a sensitive product to be treated differently from other products. It was agreed that imports of cement to the EAC would attract a 55% common external tariff, to be decreased by 5% annually to allow time for the EAC member states to accumulate the efficiency necessary to sustain competition from outside the region. However, following unprecedented price increases in 2007, it was determined that the protection should be waived to allow for imports, which eventually resulted in price stability. Notwithstanding the trade surplus in Kenya, the country had an import duty on cement of 40%, which was decreased to 25% in 2008/09.

Protection has been important in reducing the pressure of competition from deep-sea imports. However, if there had been vigorous competition within and across the countries studied here, then deep-sea imports would have played a less important role.

Industry associations

Industry associations are not part of government regulation, but they are important institutions for producers that engage government on the regulatory environment as well as lobbying for support. In addition to these roles, industry associations can be used to facilitate cartel conduct in a number of ways. Cartel meetings can be held under the auspices of the association. In addition, competition-sensitive information can be shared by players in an industry, an arrangement that is designed to increase transparency and therefore bring stability to a cartel arrangement. The information exchange arrangements in themselves can constitute a coördinated practice.

The role that industry associations can play has been clearly illustrated by the cement cartel, which operated across the whole of the SACU. The operation of the cartel was integrally tied up with the C&CI, an industry association ostensibly responsible for advancing common industry concerns and not for colluding.

Cement producers in Kenya and Tanzania belong to the EACPA, which also includes producers from Burundi, Rwanda and Uganda. There are country chapters in each of the countries. Through their association, manufacturers have commissioned a research company to conduct studies related to technology and challenges facing the cement industry. One such study was to create a 'level playing field' for cement manufacturers. The study was commissioned to give manufacturers facts on cement market dynamics, which was eventually used as a tool to advocate their positions on different platforms, including government bodies. According to the report, the main challenges facing the industry include high energy costs, transportation costs, cheap imported cement, subsidised imported cement and under-declaration at the point of entry.

Conclusion

This assessment of the cement industry across Botswana, Kenya, Namibia, South Africa, Tanzania and Zambia shows it to be a tight oligopoly, with a small number of producers controlling operations across countries and smaller, fringe independent suppliers. The nature of competition has significant implications for the market outcomes. Prices and profit margins have been very high in some countries, especially Zambia, and for much of the period in Kenya. Tanzania appears to have used openness to deep-sea imports from 2008 onwards to discipline prices.

Until 2009, the cement industry in the SACU was effectively run by a cartel, after which more competitive behaviour was evident. (It should be noted, however, that vigorous competition does not necessarily happen straight after the ending of cartel arrangements (see Khumalo et al. 2014)). A comparison of the higher margins of PPC with those before and after the cement cartel suggests cartel mark-ups of around 15 to 20 per cent over competitive prices. This is in the same ballpark as the assessment made by Hüschelrath et al. (2013) of the German cement cartel of overcharges in a range from 20.3 to 26.5 per cent. The implication is that coordinated conduct would have had a substantial harmful impact on the economies in the study where it occurred.

The study also highlights the importance of understanding investment decisions and arrangements regarding regional trade in order to assess the nature and extent of competition. Opening borders and increased investment in the region means greater competition on the whole, while firms have a strong incentive to lobby for trade protection as part of coordinating and/or to use borders as convenient ways to forego competing by instead exporting to countries in which there are no cement producers. The study shows that cement companies may operate in different regions either through the exportation of cement to those regions, or by establishing plants. Cement is produced by multinational companies that develop strategies on a wider regional basis rather than on a country-by-country basis. Any assessment of the cement industry therefore cannot be limited to the individual countries, but must be conducted from a broader geographical basis.

The cement cartel that was uncovered in South Africa in 2009 cartelised the SACU region as a whole, providing a powerful case study of how collusion can operate. The cartelists shared highly disaggregated data on a monthly, and in some instances weekly, basis. Whether other industry associations could be using a similar modus operandi to cartelise their markets, is a question that needs to be asked.

With regard to new entry, all the countries covered in the study have been experiencing entry by totally new players and also more established multinationals. This entry has brought substantially lower reported prices across the countries. For example, the entry of Dangote's Sephaku business into South Africa reduced prices and PPC's margins further after the end of the cartel in 2009 (Figures 2.5 and 2.6). In Kenya, prices were reported to have fallen to 575 Kenyan Shillings on an ex-factory basis (or around US$5.60/bag) in September 2015 due to stiff competition.[23] In Zambia, prices have also fallen substantially following entry by Dangote, with wholesale prices in June 2015 reported to be 58 Zambian Kwacha (US$7.80) on a wholesale basis.[23] In this regard it is interesting to note that the entrants are mostly not the same firms simply expanding operations, but include those new to the region. These new entrants are also constructing significant production facilities.

Finally, the study highlights the need for competition authorities to work together if they are to be able to appreciate the possible regional and international dimensions of anticompetitive arrangements.

Notes

1 Competition Commission referral, February 2015, against NPC-Cimpor, Pretoria Portland Cement, AfriSam and Lafarge, Case 2008Jun3769, available from Competition Commission South Africa on request

2 Competition Commission South Africa press release of 11 November 2009, 'PPC confesses to being part of a cement cartel and gets conditional leniency', and confirmation of the consent agreement between the Competition Commission and AfriSam (South Africa) Pty Ltd, confirmed on 16 November 2011 and available on www.comptrib.co.za

3 These additives come in different forms and they include gypsum, blast furnace slag, fly ash, silica fume, lime or limestone, and aggregates.

4 Data from the Tanzania Revenue Authority, 2010

5 It should also be noted that the Kenyan prices have been calculated from per tonne prices and therefore do not take into account bagging costs, which would possibly increase the prices further.

6 For the details, see the Competition Commission of South Africa's press release of 11 November 2009, 'PPC confesses to being part of a cement cartel and gets conditional leniency', and confirmation of the consent agreement between the Competition Commission and AfriSam (South Africa) Pty Ltd, confirmed on 16 November 2011 and available on www.comptrib.co.za

7 Confirmation of the consent agreement between the Competition Commission and AfriSam (South Africa) Pty Ltd, confirmed by the Competition Tribunal on 16 November 2011 and available on www.comptrib.co.za

8 See the Competition Commission of South Africa's press release of 11 November 2009, 'PPC confesses to being part of a cement cartel and gets conditional leniency'

9 AfriSam consent agreement, para 3.3.2 and 3.3.3; see also confirmation of the consent agreement between the Competition Commission and Lafarge Industry South Africa, confirmed by the Competition Tribunal on 28 March 2012 and available on www.comptrib.co.za

10 See the Competition Commission of South Africa's press release of 11 November 2009, 'PPC confesses to being part of a cement cartel and gets conditional leniency'

11 It still holds a small shareholding of some 3%, but no longer has a director. See http://www.reuters.com/article/2009/10/21/bamburi-athiriver-idUSLL19772920091021

12 See, for example, the rebuttable presumption in Section 21(5) of the Competition Act of Kenya of 2009 and Section 4(2) of the South African Competition Act of 1998.

13 The other entrant, Savannah Cement, apparently operates in an export-processing zone and is restricted from selling more than 20 per cent into the EAC market. See http://www.theeastafrican.co.ke/business/Why-cement-companies-are-kicking-up-dust-over-Savannah/-/2560/1913490/-/14d7r8u/-/index.html

14 See, for example, The East African 'New players changing the game in cement industry', 12 June 2011.

15 See http://www.constructionkenya.com/3007/cement-prices-kenya-drop-12-year-low-fall/

16 Lafarge Zambia annual reports

17 Approximately 1.5 tonnes of limestone are required to produce 1 tonne of cement.

18 See Sephaku Holding's financial statements for the 2009 financial year, accessed at http://www.sephakuholdings.co.za/investors.html.

19 See Hüschelrath et al. (2013) for a discussion of the most recent German cartel, in which all three were involved.

20 In Zambia, the Competition and Consumer Protection Act defines unilateral dominance as constituting 30% of market share.

21 Tanzania Investment Centre, 2010

22 See http://www.businessdailyafrica.com/Stiff-competition-keeps-cement-prices-down/-/539552/2868566/-/18fqc2/-/index.html

23 See https://www.lusakatimes.com/2015/06/29/cement-prices-start-falling-after-dongote-cement-enters-the-market/

References

Connor JM & Helmers CJ (2006) *Statistics on modern private international cartels 1990–2005.* Working Paper #06–11, Department of Agricultural Economics, Purdue University

Hüschelrath K, Müller K & Veith T (2013) Concrete shoes for competition: the effect of the German cement cartel on market price *Journal of Competition Law and Economics.* 9(1): 97–123

Khumalo, J, Mashiane J & Roberts S (2014) Harm and Overcharge in the South African Precast Concrete Products Cartel. *Journal of Competition Law and Economics.* 10(3): 621–646

Majenge, B (2012) Breakthrough in cement. *Competition News* 42. Accessed July 2013. http://www.compcom.co.za/wp-content/uploads/2014/09/Comp-Com-Newsletter-March-2012.pdf

3 *Agricultural development, competition and investment: The case of sugar in Kenya, South Africa, Tanzania and Zambia*

Brian Chisanga, John Gathiaka, George Nguruse, Stellah Onyancha and Thando Vilakazi

The sugar industry within the southern and East Africa region is an important one for agricultural development (SADC 2009). The sugar industries in each of the focus countries – Kenya, South Africa, Tanzania and Zambia – are well established and, aside from Kenya, are dominated by large multinational sugar milling companies. However, the performance across the four countries has differed substantially since 2002. Zambia and South Africa are relatively competitive net exporters; but while Zambia's exports have been increasing, South Africa's have been declining. Kenya and Tanzania are both net importers and neither recorded any sustained growth in output between 2005 and 2012.

Sugar is a widely traded agricultural commodity and international prices are very important for local industries, whether they are net exporters or importers. In the past the world sugar market has, been highly distorted by protectionism and agricultural policies in developed countries. This has been matched by protection of the sugar markets in developing countries, including the four included in the study, which is the subject of this chapter. Changes in agricultural policy, in the European Union in particular, and the progressive liberalisation of trade, have led to a less distorted international market, while some least developed countries continue to have preferential access to EU markets (EC 2013). The outcomes observed in each country are partly a reflection of the domestic policies adopted in the context of international developments, as well as the conduct of the major firms.

As monopsonistic buyers of sugar cane, sugar milling firms act as the fulcrum of the domestic sugar value chain. At the same time, investments by sugar mills in large-scale capacity are critical to ensure that sugar cane can be processed efficiently, as without this there would be no buyers for the sugar cane farmers. Millers and farmers therefore are closely tied together. For example, better farming practices mean sugar cane with higher yields of sucrose. In turn, more efficient milling means that a given sugar cane crop will be converted into more and better-quality sugar, resulting in higher revenue.

The substantial scale economies in sugar milling signify that this is generally a concentrated sector. In addition, two main multinational firms with South African roots, Illovo Sugar Ltd and the Tongaat Hulett Group, have expanded across southern Africa, although intraregional trade remains relatively low. The relationships between sugar milling companies and governments, the companies' control over investment patterns in the industry, and their market power (whether held by a single firm or a group of firms in the form of tacit coordination) are factors that are central to the pricing and supply of sugar.

In the remaining part of this introductory section, an overview of sugar production is provided. The rest of the chapter is based on the findings of the study, which looked at the sugar industry in the four countries. Data are drawn mainly from publicly available sources such as the national statistics authorities and sugar boards, and interviews with market participants. The chapter looks more closely at the main patterns of production and productivity; the major sugar milling firms and barriers to entry; developments in the specific countries; sugar pricing and regional trade; the nature and extent of competition; and the issues of competition law that have arisen in different countries.

Overview of sugar production

In all four countries, sugar is produced from crushing and refining sugar cane. Sugar is produced in a sugar cane mill when cane juice is extracted from sugar cane through the cane-crushing process to produce raw sugar, which, at this stage is not fit for human consumption. Following this, impurities, most of the molasses and foreign particles are removed and the remaining juice is then crystallised into granular brown sugar, which is further refined to produce refined (white) sugar. Generally, brown and white sugars are used by both household consumers (direct consumption) and manufacturers, such as those in the baking, confectionery, beverage and food processing industries (industrial consumption).[1]

Both the cost of production and the quality of sugar cane are critical to sugar production. Sugar cane is a relatively low-value, bulky crop, meaning that the costs to transport it are substantial. Ideally then, sugar cane is grown close to the mill. High-quality cane has good juice content with high sugar levels. The efficiency with which juice can be extracted from the cane is limited by the quality of cane delivered and the technology used. The yield of harvested cane can also be improved by ensuring that the cane is crushed as soon as possible after it has been cut. Together with the cost of transport, this means that substantial emphasis is placed on ensuring that the systems for the delivery of cane to a particular mill are effective, in terms of both time and distance. As the millers are the only potential buyers of cane and require large volumes of cane to be delivered reliably, coordination between the sugar cane growers and the millers is crucial for the industry's performance.

Typically, there are two types of arrangements for the agricultural production and supply of sugar cane: nucleus estates owned by the millers themselves, and out-growers, who are independent farmers that produce sugar cane and sell it to millers. A high proportion of out-growers signifies that there may be greater risks for the millers in terms of ensuring a steady supply of sugar cane, especially where there are many small farmers. However, independent out-growers also assume the risks and costs of farming. Where millers have a substantial nucleus estate, on the other hand, they can make investments and control the farming practices that affect the productivity of operations. In Kenya and South Africa, out-growers provide just over 90% of the crushed cane to the millers, in contrast to Zambia, where the proportion is just 40%.[2] In Tanzania, out-growers provide nearly 80% of cane.

Sugar production and productivity

The study from which the analysis is made possible covered the period from 2005 to 2012. Of the four countries studied, the largest sugar producer is South Africa, followed by Kenya, while the most rapid growth over the period 2005 to 2012 is in Zambia (see Table 3.1). Production in Zambia increased by 50%, from the level of around 260 000 tonnes from 2006 to 2008 to around 400 000 tonnes from 2011 to 2012. Production volumes in the other countries fluctuated over the period.

Table 3.1 *Domestic consumption and domestic production of sugar, 2005–2012*

	Kenya		South Africa		Tanzania		Zambia	
Year	**Volume (tonnes)**	**Volume produced, % of domestic consumption**	**Volume (tonnes)**	**Volume produced, % of domestic consumption**	**Volume (tonnes)**	**Volume produced, % of domestic consumption**	**Volume (tonnes)**	**Volume produced, % of domestic consumption**
2005	488 997	70	2 226 869	176	229 617	70	248 222	201
2006	475 670	66	2 500 504	188	263 317	77	263 451	243
2007	520 404	70	2 226 853	165	192 095	52	266 347	223
2008	517 667	69	2 273 499	167	265 434	69	261 713	184
2009	548 207	72	2 260 244	158	279 850	71	219 444	153
2010	523 207	68	2 178 450	145	263 461	66	333 304	227
2011	490 210	63	1 909 236	123	304 135	89	407 326	248
2012	578 615	72	1 822 488	108	262 879	60	398 694	235

Source: Researchers' compilation from country data, 2013

In terms of trade, Tanzania and Kenya have maintained significant trade deficits, equivalent to 30 to 40% of domestic demand. South Africa[3] has had a substantial though diminishing trade surplus, while Zambia's trade surplus has grown, with expansion in output recorded and approximately two-thirds of production being for export. This suggests that there could be high levels of intraregional trade, as Kenya and Tanzania could import from countries such as South Africa and Zambia.[4]

Some of the differences in the milling output and competitiveness of each country can be explained by variations in the overall efficiency and productivity of millers. There are also notable differences in yields in the agricultural production of cane. These reflect the arrangements between millers and farmers, and the investments at each level.

Zambian and South African sugar mills have been more productive, crushing smaller volumes of cane to yield a tonne of sugar, at 8.10 tonnes and 8.35 tonnes of cane, respectively.[5] In Kenya and Tanzania, on the other hand, on average 10.74 tonnes and 9.93 tonnes of cane were crushed respectively, to yield a tonne of refined sugar. This means the use of around 25% more cane than Zambia and South Africa.[6] As well as reflecting the efficiency of millers, the differences also reflect growing practices and transport arrangements, which both affect the sucrose content of the cane.

Zambia has also been by far the most productive country in terms of sugar cane farmed, with an estimated 106.2 tonnes of sugar cane produced per hectare in 2012, compared with just 63.4t/ha for Kenya in 2011, 62.1t/ha in South Africa in 2011/12[7] and between 30 and 60 t/ha for Tanzania[8].

Productivity in Kenya had been declining for several years, apparently due to ageing machinery, low reinvestment in improved technologies, frequent mill breakdowns, and poor maintenance programmes, particularly at older mills. The reasons that this has been allowed to happen are not clear, although it is worth noting that newer mills have been making significant investments in up-to-date technologies, trucks, machinery, and weighbridges that are close to the farms.

At the other extreme, in Zambia the high productivity at the levels of both agricultural production and sugar yields from cane are the result of substantial investments by Zambia Sugar, which is discussed further below.

Scale economies in milling and the transporting of cane signify that mills are generally located in areas of sugar cane production. Transporting cane effectively means transporting ten times the weight of the sugar produced from that cane, which is extremely bulky. Coordination of the milling capacity with cane growing is also important to ensure that the factories have a consistent stream of raw material so that they are able to operate as close to full capacity as possible. The quality of the cane also impacts on the yields that can be achieved. In addition, growers need to know that they have a market for their cane.

The shared interests of growers and millers

The shared interests of farmers and millers signify that there are typically exclusive vertical agreements for cane supply, where the millers source from independent growers.

These agreements can range from one season to 50 years, with effective exclusivity. In Kenya, South Africa and Tanzania, there are similar vertical arrangements in terms of cane supply arrangements between growers and millers, and these are governed by the relevant laws and regulations in each country. Contracts are typically negotiated between individual millers and growers. In Zambia, the largest producer, Zambia Sugar, sources most of its cane from its own nucleus estates. This is supplemented by sourcing from growers with which it has established vertical relationships that are governed by exclusive contractual arrangements.

In addition to growers entering into supply agreements with millers for the certainty that their cane will be processed, in some instances millers offer some form of financial, technical or developmental assistance to the grower in exchange for an exclusive cane supply agreement.

The joint interests of growers and millers have meant that, in each country, the sugar cane price is based on a formula for sharing the price of sugar between the miller and the cane grower, coupled with provisions for the quality of the cane delivered. The quality is measured by Estimated Recoverable Crystals (ERC) of cane delivered by a grower for crushing. The arrangements for dividing the proceeds recognise the fact that growers often do not have a choice in terms of where they can feasibly deliver their sugar cane, given the higher transport costs if they were looking to sell to a mill further afield. In other words, in the short term, the millers effectively have buyer power over sugar farmers. However, if growers do not invest in their crop then the mill will not have sufficient quantity and quality of cane to operate efficiently. Therefore, in the medium to longer term, there is a mutual interest in higher-quality cane being grown, with millers obviously relying on farmers for their inputs. There is a need for coordination to ensure investment that benefit both the farming and milling sectors.

The bulky nature of cane and its relatively low value mean that transport costs can be high. Transport costs range from approximately 12% of growers' costs in South Africa, to 23% in Tanzania and 29% in Zambia.[9] In the case of Kenya, the transportation of cane is arranged by the millers themselves and that cost is then passed on to the grower in the form of deductions from the amount the mill pays to the growers. This means that the costs of poorly organised transport can be passed onto the farmers, thus undermining the incentives to coordinate effectively.

The situation in Kenya for the period 2005 to 2012 shows what happens when the relationships between growers and millers break down. The inefficiencies of the older mills, including the poor organisation of transport and late and irregular payment of farmers, signify erratic supply, which, in turn, reduces the ability of millers to operate at optimal levels. There has also been low absorption of new farming technologies. Some newer mills were established in sugar-growing areas and were effectively competing with the older and less efficient mills for cane. New mills tend to pay weekly and provide support and advice to farmers. Overall, however, the necessary restructuring to more efficient and modern production was not coordinated, which means that that overall milling capacity far outstripped cane production and older mills continued operating at very low levels of capacity utilisation. In addition, as millers looked to attract growers to deliver cane to their mills, they offered higher cane prices, which raised the mills' operating costs. Furthermore, even though growers received higher prices for their cane as a result, they still seemed to operate in a high-cost environment due to the poor use of new farming technologies and bad payment practices by older mills.

In Tanzania, the division of proceeds agreement in the industry stipulated that proceeds from sugar production and sales should be divided between growers and millers at a ratio of 60:40. This ratio was never actually achieved, however, over the period studied and stood at around 53 to 56.5% to growers in 2012 to 2013, rather than 60% (Sugar Board of Tanzania 2013). There were also problems with cane supply. For example, declines in production had arisen at the Mtibwa Sugar Estate because of strained relationships between growers and millers. In extreme cases, some growers decided to switch from sugar cane production to other agricultural produce, with out-growers complaining about the low prices paid by millers and the delayed payment of proceeds. This situation was exacerbated by unpredictable weather conditions and the fact that the low sugar cane prices meant that farmers invested less in fertilizer and herbicides (Sugar Board of Tanzania 2013). It is worth noting that both Tanzania and Kenya remain net importers of sugar products, which may be a direct result of the kind of difficulties outlined above.

In South Africa, the ratio for the division of proceeds has been about 63:37 in favour of growers; and in Zambia from 2012 to 2013 it was 59:41 in favour of growers. However, cane supply in South Africa has been constrained by severe drought conditions over several years and uncertainty relating to the land claims process.[10] The drought conditions have resulted in the largest milling company in South Africa (Illovo) having to intermittently close down one of its mills and divert cane to another mill.[11] By comparison, Zambia grew its production of cane and sugar, capitalising on favourable local conditions for sugar production, although the long distances to major export markets reduce the net returns that can be made.

The major firms and barriers to entry

The firms

Concentration in sugar production has been relatively high across the four countries. The Zambian sugar industry is the most concentrated, with only three milling companies, of which Zambia Sugar (owned by Illovo) has had a share in excess of 90%. In Tanzania there have been two substantial producers, Kilombero and TPC Limited, with a collective share of around 70%, and several smaller producers. Kilombero is controlled by Illovo[12], while Sukari Investments from Mauritius holds 75% of TPC.

Moreover, the other two established firms in the industry, Mtibwa and Kagera, have been co-owned by the same two individuals.[13] South Africa has three producers – Illovo, TSB and Tongaat-Hulett – with shares over the period of around 25 to 30% each. By comparison, Kenya had seven local producers in 2012, with shares of between 5 and 15% each. Only one of the older mills, Mumias, had a share above 30%.

Illovo is the largest firm in the region and controls substantial sugar interests across six countries, with an overwhelming dominant position in two of them. Illovo has been controlled by Associated British Foods since its acquisition of a 51% stake in 2006. The Illovo sugar estate was established in South Africa in the late 19th century, and in the 1970s it was consolidated under the CG Smith group, which acquired the Illovo Group from the British sugar company Tate and Lyle.[14] In the late 1990s, Illovo started to expand across southern and East Africa. In 1997, Illovo acquired the Lonrho sugar interests in South Africa, Mauritius, Swaziland and Malawi, and in 1998 Illovo acquired Kilombero Sugar in Tanzania (the Mauritius interests were sold in 2001). In 1999, Illovo's Maragra mill opened in Mozambique and in 2001, the firm acquired Zambia Sugar. Illovo has accounted for close to 100% of production in Malawi and Zambia, and between 30% and 40% in South Africa, Tanzania and Swaziland, while its share in Mozambique has been relatively small.[15]

A total of 1.7 million tonnes of sugar was produced by Illovo in 2013, yielding total revenue of ZAR11.1 billion and an operating profit of R1.9 billion. The contributions of the different countries to revenue and profit varied substantially, however. While South Africa accounted for 38% of the revenue in the 2013 financial year, it accounted for just 8.6% of the operating profit. At the other extreme is Malawi, with 16.4% of the revenue and 47.3% of the operating profit, followed by Zambia, which accounted for 22.6% of the revenue and 25.2% of the profit.[16] As noted above, Zambia has seen substantial investments in capacity and technology since 2006 on the part of Zambia Sugar, while there have also been major investments by Illovo in other countries, including South Africa and Tanzania.

The second-largest producer in the region is Tongaat Hulett, which produced 1.3 million tonnes of sugar in 2013. The company has four mills in South Africa, two mills in Mozambique and mills in Swaziland and Zimbabwe. In the 2013 financial year, Tongaat Hulett's total revenue was R14.4 billion, with an operating profit of R2.1 billion. It also has distribution centres in Botswana and Namibia. The company's sugar production has grown strongly in Mozambique, while volumes recovered in South Africa and Zimbabwe in 2013 and 2014 after declines in previous years. However, total production across the countries remained substantially below the milling capacity of 2.1 million tonnes. Although the company's Swaziland operations are small, these have the highest margins or operating profits out of revenue – with 37% in 2013, followed by Mozambique with 25% and Zimbabwe with 19%.[17] Margins in South Africa were just 7% in 2013.[18]

Barriers to entry

Barriers to entry at the milling level of the sugar industry are substantial. Achieving significant economies of scale means large investments have to be made to achieve efficient processing costs. Achieving scale production also requires simultaneous investments in sugar cane farming, which requires a lot of water. Together, this implies considerable planning and capital expenditure over a number of years to ensure coordination before full production comes on-stream.[19] Shortages of sugar cane supply have affected the milling operations in both South Africa and Kenya, and resulted in increased average costs.

Other barriers to entry have included the regulatory environment in each country and the existing relationships between governments and the incumbent large milling companies. These have served to align the incentives of government and millers such that new entrants find it difficult to compete with incumbents and to enjoy the same support in establishing operations as the incumbents.

Despite these barriers, smaller private operators have entered Kenya and Tanzania. Kenya has a large number of sugar cane producers dispersed throughout the country with state support, while Tanzania has targeted sugar as a source of agricultural growth and has aimed to attract investors. Zambia and South Africa have not experienced the entry of new competitors for several years, even though, in the case of Zambia, profit margins have been relatively high and sustained.

Country-specific developments

Kenya

Sugar-milling companies in Kenya have historically been state owned, following a strategy by the Kenyan government to increase socio-economic activity in the rural areas (Kenya Sugar Board 2009: 30). However, this has meant relatively low levels of productivity due to poor management under state ownership, which led to a change in approach, including the privatisation of the largest mill, Mumias, and the opening up of the industry to private entrants. Mumias showed better productive performance after privatisation relative to the remaining state-owned mills.

Additional licences were issued to new millers. This may have been because the price of sugar in Kenya was very high, making the market attractive to entrant millers. Three new millers entered the market between 2008 and 2013. The new entrants did, however, lead to concerns about overcapacity and whether they would be able to establish the scale of operations required to affect pricing and allow for the expansion of production output. Most of the existing factories were already operating below capacity, due to several factors, ranging from cane shortages to the breakdown of machinery. Overall, the decline in the production efficiency in the Kenyan sugar industry has been largely due to ageing and badly maintained machinery.

The combination of increased milling capacity and poor farming performance has led to shortages of sugar cane, which have had dramatic effects on some of the milling companies. For instance, capacity utilisation at Mumias – which has had the largest installed crushing capacity in Kenya – dropped from 98% in the period up to 2010 to 83% in 2011, and then to 55% in 2012. Sugar output from this factory declined, while factory overheads increased. Historically, Mumias has been the producer with the lowest cost base due to its use of diffuser technology to extract sugar. Interestingly, by comparison, West Kenya, which is one of the private millers with a strong market position in Kenya, has expanded with investments in Uganda and Tanzania.

The problem of excess capacity has been exacerbated by technical and management constraints that have further limited the domestic production of sugar and denied the factories the benefits of economies of scale. It appears that the millers have had to offer higher prices to growers for sugar cane such that the prices for sugar cane in the market are also likely to be inflated.

Finally, Kenya's sugar shortage is usually met by imports. However, in 2011, government delays in facilitating imports pertaining to the Common Market for Eastern and Southern Africa (COMESA) quota exacerbated the upward pricing effects in this market (COMESA 2012). Furthermore, the multiplicity of domestic and trade regulations, the subsequent amendment of these regulations, the poor integration between different laws and regulations, and the subjective vetting of import permit applicants have constrained the administration of sugar imports and the efficiency of the domestic market. Collectively, these are non-tariff barriers that have served to constrain regional trade in sugar.

Tanzania

As with Kenya, Tanzania has maintained a trade deficit as domestic sugar supply has failed to match demand. The sugar industry was run by the state until the liberalisation of the sugar trade in 1992 and the privatisation of the sugar companies, starting with Kilombero in 1997/98, Mtibwa in 1998/99, TPC in 2000/01 and finally Kagera in 2001/02.[20]

There were substantial capital investments at the end of the 1990s. According to the Association of Millers, investments totalling US$500 million increased the total milling capacity from 98 000 tonnes before privatisation in 1998 to over 300 000 tonnes in 2013. However, as Table 3.1 shows, output between 2005 and 2012 did not record sustained growth to match the capacity expansion. In 2013 and 2014, actual production remained just under 300 000 tonnes.[21] Investments by millers have focused on ensuring sugar cane supply and improving the current efficiency of existing milling operations, such as methods to ensure sustainable mill electrification and workers' conditions of employment.

Further substantial investments were planned in 2013 and 2014, which would see a significant change to Tanzania being a net sugar exporter. In April 2013, the

Sugar Board of Tanzania outlined nine sugar production projects. The projects' implementation would see the country tripling its annual sugar production from close to 300 000 tonnes to over 900 000 tonnes, taking advantage of expected agricultural yields of cane per hectare that were at least as good as in Zambia.[22] This plan included the provision of tax and other investment incentives in order to attract foreign direct investment (TIC 2010). Interestingly, some of these tax incentives are very similar to those that Zambia Sugar (Illovo) has been accused of misusing in Zambia, as described in Lewis (2013).

The local supply and pricing of sugar in Tanzania has apparently been influenced by the particular distribution arrangements of the two largest sugar producers. TPC, which has one plant in the north-eastern part of the country, distributes sugar through contracted agents where a written contract has restricted agents from trading competing brands and required the agent to sell at a specified location. Adherence to these requirements has been closely monitored and TPC has thus been easily able to control supply and the market price. Kilombero distributes its sugar through a marketing company called Kilombero Sugar Distributor Company (KSDC), which handles all its marketing activities. Over 80% of the sugar marketed by KSDC has been sold to two private dealers and, to a large extent, these dealers have determined the amount and therefore the market price for large proportions of the country. The remaining sugar has been sold directly to large wholesalers. The prices offered to the large wholesalers for buying from KSDC have been higher than the price offered to the two main dealers. Therefore, a great deal of market power has been vested in these two dealers at the distribution level, compared to a country like South Africa, where there are several different routes to market.

South Africa

The South African sugar industry is highly regulated. The South African Sugar Association (SASA) is mandated by the Sugar Act of 1978 to maintain a network of provisions designed to 'protect' the domestic industry. It does this in four main ways. First, SASA estimates the amount of sugar that will be required by the local market based on consumer demand. Then, through the single export desk, SASA ensures that surplus sugar is removed from the market to prevent excess supply and 'destructive' domestic market competition from driving prices down to export parity.

Second, domestic market entitlements are allocated to each miller based on the volume of saleable sugar produced in the previous season.

Third, a flexible market share system allows firms to sell more sugar in the domestic market than their pro-rata share of total production (that is, their entitlement) and in turn compensates those firms that effectively 'diverted' their share to the lower-priced export market. When a firm has 'oversold' in the domestic market, it must pay over to SASA an amount that is calculated as the volume of the sugar oversold in the domestic market multiplied by the weighted average of the notional price (discussed below) less a manufacturing allowance and export realisation. This amount is redistributed to domestically 'underselling' firms as compensation on a quarterly basis.

Finally, with input from both producers and growers, SASA determines a notional price for sugar, which serves as a reference price for the determination of the proceeds sharing between sugar producers and growers. It is important to point out that this notional price is not equivalent to the selling price nor is it a maximum price for sugar in the domestic market as producers are free to price above this level. According to SASA, the decision to sell sugar at a price that is above or below the local notional price rests solely with the individual milling companies.

This system has ensured that firms are incentivised to sell locally until the price is at the notional price and then, rather than the local price being depressed further, sales are channelled into the export market. As the entitlements of each miller to the domestic market are based on their contribution to total industry production (and not sales) in the first place, millers can compete on that basis for a larger share of the market. This type of competition might take the form of increased levels of investment in capacity and efficiency-enhancing technologies. The geographical constraints that exist in terms of sourcing sugar cane from long distances within South Africa, as well as constraints relating to water availability, have made it unusual for this level of competition to take place, because it may not actually be economically feasible to compete for cane supply that is located very far from the mill. Coupled with the compensation mechanism, any likelihood of real competition between millers is diminished, at least in terms of volumes of cane sourced and crushed.

It is unsurprising that the market shares of sugar companies in South Africa have remained relatively stable since 2005, despite the adverse weather conditions, including droughts in 2011 and 2012. The regulatory environment effectively undermines competition between millers in the sugar market, while cane supply agreements are able to protect millers from direct competition for cane. The impact of the system depends heavily on how the notional price is determined. The determination of the notional price has in fact meant relatively good prices for South African consumers over the period under review.

Zambia

Sugar trade in Zambia was liberalised in 1990. The main producer, Zambia Sugar, was privatised in 1995 and subsequently acquired by Illovo in 2001. National capacity and output doubled from around 200 000 tonnes per year in 2002 to more than 400 000 tonnes in 2012.[23] The doubling of production can be attributed to expansion led by Zambia Sugar. In 2006, Zambia Sugar embarked on a massive expansion of estates and plant capacity, which saw the company's installed capacity increase to 450 000 tonnes per year.[24] While local demand increased with strong economic growth, the scale of the expansion meant that increased production largely went into export markets.

Zambian legislation requires all sugar for direct consumption in the domestic market to be fortified with Vitamin A in specific quantities.[25] As part of an initiative of the government through the Ministry of Health and the USAID Micronutrient Programme, the legislation, which came into effect in 2000, was motivated by the need to increase the availability of Vitamin A to the population. Zambia Sugar has embraced the fortification initiative. This has also served to control the influx of cheap imported sugar to the Zambian market at a time when Zambia Sugar had started feeling pressure from legal and illegal imports of sugar from Malawi and Zimbabwe in amounts estimated to have reached 25% of Zambia's domestic market (Serlemistos & Fusco 2010). The USAID Micronutrient Programme, however, observed that the legislation had the potential to entrench Zambia Sugar as a monopoly, thus effectively reducing competition from imports and distorting the domestic industry (Serlemistos & Fusco 2010).

This legislation does not exist in most countries and, together with the requirement for import licences, it has effectively blocked potential imports from entering Zambia. In addition to this legislation, there are administrative barriers to sugar imports, including high tariff rates on imported sugar from outside the trading blocs of which the country is a member. These rates have surpassed the rate commonly applied to most finished products (WTO 2007). Potential importers are also required to obtain import permits from the government, but the process is not transparent and is often delayed (Chisanga et al. 2014). In addition, imports have to be cleared by three ministries (the Ministry of Agriculture and Livestock, the Ministry of Health and the Ministry of Commerce, Trade and Industry). The effect of these non-tariff barriers is evident in the negligible level of sugar imports of both direct consumption and industrial sugars. Together with the various barriers to importing, Zambia Sugar as the dominant producer has had the ability to set domestic sugar prices at relatively high levels, even when Zambia is a low-cost sugar producer (Nyberg 2011).

Sugar pricing and trade

Pricing in each country

In all the countries covered in the study, ex-factory prices for sugar have been higher than the world prices (Figure 3.1).[26] Ex-factory prices are the prices for a commodity at the factory gate, net of all discounts and rebates, generally for bulk sales.[27] It is to be expected that these prices would be higher than the world price for net-importing countries like Tanzania and Kenya, which incur transport costs for imports, and which do not have a comparative advantage in sugar. By comparison, for net-exporting countries with competitive industries, such as Zambia and South Africa, high local prices potentially signify the existence of regulation and/or some exercise of market power. The world price in the sugar industry, however, may not be a good benchmark for comparison. This is because, at least until 2006 (when there was a 25-year spike in the world price), the world price for sugar was viewed as artificially low, due to the subsidisation of large, inefficient producers in Europe and elsewhere, which distorted world prices (Nyberg 2011). Since 2006, the EU has progressively phased out these subsidies, although extensive support remains in other countries such as the USA.

Of the four countries covered in the study, Kenya has had the highest ex-factory prices, followed by Zambia, while Tanzania and South Africa have had relatively lower ex-factory prices. It should be noted also that Tanzania only produces brown sugar (and imports white sugar), which is less costly to produce as less refinement is required. Typically, the difference between the prices of white and brown sugar is approximately 10% or less (based on estimates from South Africa). So, to be comparable with average prices of white and brown sugar in the other countries, an adjustment of less than 10% could be made to the Tanzanian prices. But even with this adjustment, from 2005 to 2011, the price of sugar in Tanzania has in most years been lower than prices in Kenya and Zambia. There are also typically lower prices for industrial sugar than the benchmark household white and brown sugar on which price data have been sourced.

Figure 3.1 *Ex-factory and world sugar prices (US$/tonne)*

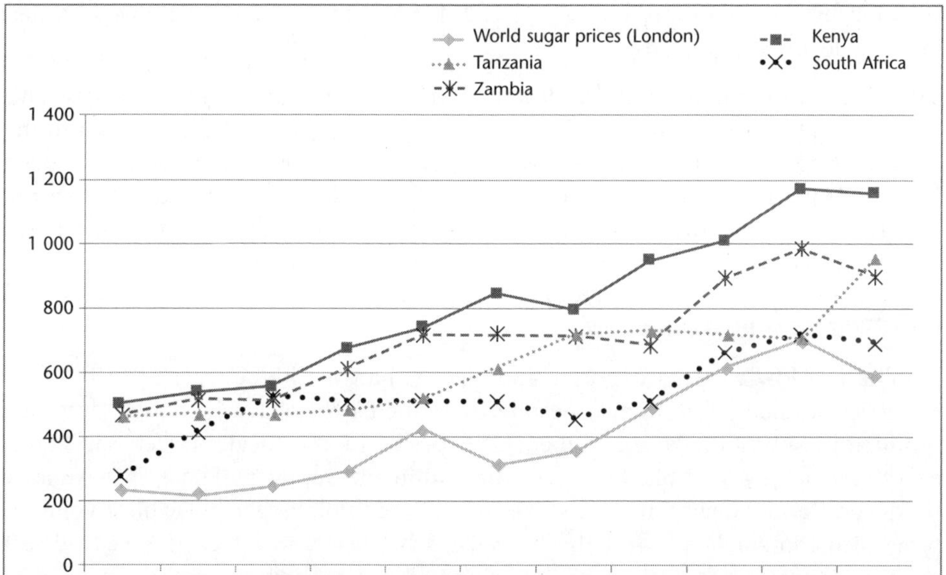

Source: Researchers' compilation from country data, 2013

The ex-factory price can be administered or it can be set by the millers themselves, including through competition between them and against imports. In the cases of Tanzania and Zambia, the price is set by the millers. However, the supplies required to meet local demand in Tanzania include imports such that the import price, including any tariffs and duties, sets the price. In Kenya, also a net importer, there are restrictions on imports, including licences being required, and the fact that the Kenya Sugar Board (KSB) pricing committee works out ex-factory local sugar prices and makes recommendations to millers. However, the millers have indicated that the price recommendations of KSB usually have not been realistic and therefore have not been adhered to at all. The notional price in South Africa is set by the Sugar Association under the rules set down in the Sugar Act.

Prices in Kenya have thus been the highest over the period because of high levels of import protection for the domestic market, and because of the inefficiencies and high-cost nature of the local industry, which means that there has been a persistent trade deficit. In normal competitive markets one would expect that competition would erode away any excessive margins earned by millers, especially in cases such as Kenya, where there has been new entry to the market. However, because of cane shortages, production inefficiency and substantial protection against cheaper imports, prices have remained extremely high, at over 300% of the world market price, on average. In Kenya in 2011, the general shortage of sugar domestically triggered an increase in sugar prices. The government could have alleviated the situation by allowing more imports of COMESA sugar, but it only allowed limited imports during this period.

Tanzania, on the other hand, has fewer players in the market, but the prices have been lower than those of its neighbour. This is primarily because, in contrast to the situation in Kenya, Tanzania has managed its trade policy so that there have been increased imports of sugar to the market to bridge the deficit in domestic production. The Tanzanian government has also intervened at times to allow imports and it has issued indicative prices (price caps), both of which have suppressed domestic prices. At the same time, Tanzania has sought to increase domestic production capacity and the efficiency of local producers.

Zambia is a low-cost net exporter and yet has had the highest prices of the four countries studied, after Kenya, despite investments that have increased domestic production substantially since 2006. The prices in the local market have been effectively set by Zambia Sugar as the dominant supplier. There is a smaller producer, Kafue Sugar, which has priced below Zambia Sugar but whose volumes have been too small to affect the overall market price. In effect, the weak threat of imports appears to have been the ceiling on the pricing of Zambia Sugar even though imports are not required to supply the local market and there have been very substantial exports. The impact of imports is weakened by the vitamin fortification requirements and the licensing requirements on importers.

In South Africa, there is effectively government-sanctioned coordination through regulation. This appears, however, to have yielded relatively low prices compared to the other countries, although substantially above the world price in earlier years when the world price was more distorted. From 2009 to 2012, South African prices closely tracked the world sugar price and have generally been lower than those of the other countries covered in the study. These outcomes probably exist because although the country has exported a significant amount of sugar as a net exporter, the domestic price of sugar has been moderated by the fact that there are imports (mainly from Brazil), as well as the operation of regulation. As such, the pricing and margins in the domestic market have been below what one would expect to see in a typical 'cartelised' market.

Costs and margins

The major cost components of the ex-factory price at the mill are the costs of raw materials, including the purchasing of sugar cane and agricultural overhead costs. The balance comprises direct and overhead factory costs, and marketing and distribution costs. The contribution of each item to the ex-factory price varies from one factory to the other, depending on operational efficiency.

According to the KSB (2010), the main contributors to the retail price of sugar in Kenya are the farmers' production cost and mark-up (30.3% of the price), the millers' cost and mark-up (51.3%), the wholesalers' cost and mark-up (6.1%), and the retailers' cost and mark-up (12.3%). This implies that the farmers' production cost and mark-up, and millers cost and mark-up, are collectively 93.0% of the wholesale price. Given an average ex-factory (wholesale) price of US$1000/tonne in 2010 implying that the farmers' and millers' costs, including margins, were over US$900/ tonne in that year.

In Tanzania, millers' costs of production, including the costs of sugar cane, ranged from US$360/tonne to US$580/tonne, depending on the efficiency of millers, with the major cost components being sugar cane, factory overheads and marketing (Sugar Board of Tanzania 2011). This compares with the ex-factory price in 2010 and 2011 of just over US$700/tonne.

In terms of the Zambian market, a number of previous studies have made estimates of the costs of producing sugar in Zambia. In 2004, LMC International ranked Zambia as the fourth-lowest-cost sugar producer in the world, with costs ranging between US$160 and US$240/tonne. In 2006, LMC International found that Zambia was the eighth-lowest-cost sugar producer in the world, with costs ranging from US$220 to US$430/tonne (LMC International 2010). The most recent study by LMC International and the Overseas Development Institute (ODI) in 2012 placed Zambia in the low-cost bracket among African Caribbean and Pacific (ACP) sugar-producing countries. Based on these estimates and information submitted for this study, Zambia's production costs likely ranged between US$400/tonne and US$600/tonne in 2012 (LMC & ODI 2012; data from sugar millers).[28] These estimates are broadly consistent with estimates provided by market participants and are in line with costs in Tanzania, which has also been identified as a high-yield grower of sugar and low-cost producer, if the necessary investments are made (SAGCOT 2012). The costs compare with the estimated ex-factory price of sugar in Zambia at around US$910/tonne for 2012, based on data from millers.[29] This suggests that the ex-factory (operating) margins earned by millers on the basis of average factory costs and ex-factory prices in Zambia are between 34% and 56%. While this compares with the Illovo operating margins for 2012 in Zambia of 20%, this is an average margin, including the majority of volumes which are exported, where substantial transport costs to destinations as far as Europe are incurred. It also includes distribution costs and intra-group costs, such as for marketing and management services to entities registered in Ireland.

Cane procurement costs are also the most substantial production cost component of the ex-factory price of sugar in South African mills. These costs can constitute approximately 60% to 70% of the ex-factory price at some mills, followed by labour, which accounts for approximately 6% to 10%. The balance of costs is attributable to factors such as factory overheads, fuel, maintenance and packaging. Some millers estimated their operating margins for 2012 to be below 5%, while the margins of other millers could be roughly estimated to be close to 20% for some categories of customers.

In terms of operating margins and profits, it is worth noting that the information for Zambia and South Africa is broadly consistent with what can be gleaned from the annual reports of the multinational firms. Illovo has reported higher profits in Zambia than in South Africa, Tanzania or Swaziland, although Malawi, where it has 100% of the market, has had the highest margins overall. Tongaat Hulett has also reported higher margins from countries other than South Africa. This is consistent with the view that the two largest multinational firms in the regional sugar industry have raised their profits substantially from their operations in countries outside of South Africa.

Sugar trade in the region

The sugar trade in the eastern and southern African regions is governed by national, regional and international regulations and trade agreements. These agreements include the SADC trade protocol, COMESA FTA, Everything But Arms (EBA) agreement under the EU, Common Protocol for commodities in the EAC, and preferential market access under the African Growth and Opportunity Act (AGOA). Notably, Kenya and Tanzania, as members of the EAC, consider sugar to be a sensitive product, with the sector needing to be protected from import competition. This involves restrictions being imposed on imports.

In the period 2005 to 2012, Kenya imposed tariffs of 100% on imports outside COMESA in addition to VAT of 16%, while Tanzania applied tariffs of 100% in addition to VAT at 18% (although, if there is considerable shortage, common external tariff protocols are waived to allow imports at a lower tariff). Zambia restricts imports through the Vitamin A fortification requirement, as discussed above, as well as onerous and bureaucratic import licensing procedures. Zambia has also imposed tariffs on imports from outside the COMESA and SADC countries at about 23.8%. South Africa regulates its imports although only through tariffs based on the volatile world market price and the decided notional local price.

Somewhat surprisingly, there has been low trade in sugar between sugar-producing countries within the region, while there are many instances of increasing trade with countries outside the region and to non-sugar producers. In part, this reflects transport costs. For example, although it is relatively easy for Zambia to export to the neighbouring regions of the DRC the costs of sea freight, even to faraway destinations, may be lower than land freight costs to consumer markets further afield in other countries in the region.

Of the four countries, Kenya has been the largest net importer. Traditionally, Kenya has imported sugar from Egypt, Saudi Arabia, South Africa, Malawi and Madagascar. Kenya has also made small exports to the EU under the ACP countries preferential trade access, (although exports are generally marginal), as well as to Sudan, Somalia and Uganda. As a deficit market, Kenya offers a large market for sugar in the region from low-cost sugar producers, such as Zambia and Malawi. However, overland transport costs, together with the complexity of the regulatory framework, have made it difficult for sugar-exporting countries in the region and from outside of it to access the Kenyan market – underpinning the persistently high prices in Kenya's domestic market. By comparison, Tanzania has had a more open import regime, especially with the relaxation of protection in years of high international sugar prices.

South Africa and Zambia export both to the region and to the rest of the world. Regional markets for South Africa have been led by Mozambique, Zimbabwe, Angola and Madagascar, which collectively accounted for 47% of exports in 2012. This was not the case three years prior to this, when most of South Africa's exports were directed to overseas markets. Zambia exports to Europe (46% of exports in 2012) under the preferential access for ACP countries and to regional markets, led by the DRC (36% in 2012), with other smaller regional markets, such as Burundi, collectively accounting for the remainder.[30] It is important to note that even with the preferential access to the European market, the net returns from exports to Europe are estimated to be lower than local sales, due to the extensive transport costs involved (including the overland transport to the export port).

The expansion of multinational companies would be expected to influence trade flows. For example, as Illovo is dominant in Zambia and Malawi and has large stakes in Tanzania and South Africa, it would be unlikely to export from one country into another if this had the effect of competing down prices against its own businesses.

An analysis of competition concerns

The discussion above has shown that each of the domestic sugar industries is quite different in terms of the economic outcomes observed, as well as suggesting the possible reasons for the different outcomes. Regional competition dynamics also play a role, and key questions relating to competition, such as the vertical agreements between growers and millers, the extent of concentration and the impact of regulatory and other barriers to entry and expansion, are explored here. In addition to pricing, the possible links to the productivity of milling companies within each country are also examined.

To answer these questions, it is important to briefly identify the main competition problems within each country covered in the study.

The competition authorities in South Africa have generally considered the concern in the industry to be that there is a lack of dynamic competition between millers, and that this is entrenched by a regulatory structure which seeks to protect these firms. The issues related to vertical agreements between millers and growers are perhaps secondary to this, as there can be more vigorous competition among the three millers than allowed for by the regulatory structure. The evaluation in the study, however, shows that regulation has yielded fairly favourable prices for consumers in the local market, while providing a cushion to producers against the distorted world market, especially in the earlier 2000s. In other words, the regulations have been effective at constraining the pricing power of the major producers. That these companies have chosen to invest in other countries in the region reflects the capabilities they have developed in South Africa as well as the fact that South Africa, as a water-scarce country, can find more favourable growing conditions in countries such as Zambia.

Of the four countries studied, the Zambian sugar industry has perhaps been most affected by the investment behaviour of large multinationals and the fact that market power has been vested in one firm, in a protected market without a regulatory structure to constrain its pricing power. As discussed, Illovo, through Zambia Sugar, has maintained over 90% of market share and the firm has enjoyed high profitability in the Zambian market. This strong market position and high profitability have been entrenched by import protections, which have allowed the firm to strategically position itself to produce for regional and deep-sea export markets. From its operations in Zambia, Illovo has been able to leverage the benefits under the prevailing duty-free and quota-free trade regime granted to least-developed countries (LDCs) by the EU. It is important to note that the firm is a low-cost producer, due to investments in state-of-the art machinery and technology, technical expertise and world-class management, resulting in high levels of efficiency. The firm should thus be in a position to offer more competitive pricing to the Zambian domestic market and to net importers in the region. Despite this, it has been observed that the prices of sugar in Zambia do not reflect the cost advantages and high levels of productivity in that market.

The Zambian competition authority and government have alleged that there is likely to be excessive pricing in the domestic market. This is supported by the fact that the export prices are lower than the price that Zambia Sugar charges in the domestic market. Zambia Sugar is also able to sustain arrangements whereby it charges the same single national delivered price to all its depots around the country through a closely monitored network of distributors.

The competition concerns in Kenya are quite different from the other focus countries. The situation in Kenya has been that the prices of sugar are exceptionally high, despite the significant amount of new entry occurring in the market. The sector overall has been uncompetitive, with a lack of investment and poor coordination between millers and farmers. The required restructuring has also not been happening in a coordinated manner, as new entrants have set up operations without necessarily expanding cane production. The entry of new private millers using more efficient production methods could change this situation, although newly licensed private millers have been accused of 'cane poaching'. Cane poaching is a significant concern in so far as it highlights the fact that there are fundamental problems around the high costs of inputs, low cane yields, and an unreliable supply of good-quality cane. These feed through to raise millers' costs. Together with vested interests that have continued to ensure protection for the sector, the costs have seemingly been passed on to consumers in the form of very high prices.

The main competition concerns in Tanzania have arisen because of the vertical relationships between millers and distributors or wholesalers. The market is oligopolistic (with multinationals owning a majority share in the two largest producers) and there has been limited direct competition between domestic producers. This relates largely to the nature of the geographic market, whereby sugar factories are widely dispersed. Effectively, within each sugar zone in the country, millers have a network of distributors and wholesalers either through direct distribution through exclusively contracted agents or indirect distribution to agents through the millers' sister companies. The tied-up nature of the market appears to have inhibited investment and this has meant that prices are still set by imports, and the level of import protection. Further to this, it has been alleged that millers through the industry association have lobbied to limit the level of imports coming into the Tanzanian market.

At the regional level, there are substantial opportunities to grow sugar production, which needs to combine appropriate measures to support investment at both the growing and the milling levels. The division of the benefits from the production will depend on the formula governing the process. For example, in Zambia, Chisanga et al. (2014) find that growers have benefited from growing sugar revenues through the sharing of proceeds. This also supports investment at the farming level, which improves the overall efficiency of the supply chain. However, the extent to which consumers benefit depends on competition between companies within and across countries and, in the absence of effective competition, on regulation that constrains market power. The regional market has been fragmented by trade barriers, transport costs and inefficiencies, and by the lack of a coherent regional framework for developing the industry which supports investment, growth and competition.

The attractiveness of investments in the sugar industry to governments is an important factor here. The sugar industry in any country is often in a position to create a large number of jobs. This aligns the incentives of sovereign governments with those of private entities. Governments in Zambia and Tanzania, for instance, have created lucrative incentive programmes for investments in their respective sugar industries. Where the government operates as both a regulator and a substantial shareholder in milling companies, the alignment between government and the large firms can distort the nature and quality of competitiveness in those industries, as may be the case in Kenya and Tanzania. Companies earn returns from lobbying, rather than investing in productivity improvements. In Kenya, the best-performing milling companies are generally those without state ownership. Partly as a result of these sorts of distortions, Kenya and Tanzania are low-producing net importers of sugar products, whereas one might expect more dynamic competition in these domestic markets as well as regionally in East Africa.

Regulatory and other barriers to entry and expansion have substantially affected domestic productivity and regional competitiveness. Regulation, particularly with regards to the issuing of licences and protection against imports, has further entrenched firms' pricing power over local consumers even while they may be exporting.

With regards to the licensing of new producers, the governments of Tanzania and Kenya have sought to issue further licences to new milling companies. However, this is not necessarily commensurate with the ability of existing companies to remain competitive. In both of these countries, distortions within the domestic industry at different levels of the value chain have meant that mills have not been producing at close to full capacity. A key reason for this is the unevenness in the supply of quality sugar cane. Whereas the introduction of further competition may serve to increase employment and reduce prices, it may have the effect of increasing the disparities in terms of adequate cane supply and productivity. Mills may therefore face high costs of maintaining underutilised capacity such that supply is constrained and prices do not decrease as expected.

Protection and industry support is, however, a global phenomenon in the sugar industry and has had the effect of distorting the world price. In an industry with high fixed costs and high investment costs, it can be argued that it is prudent to support firms in order to allow them to achieve economies of scale. At issue is whether the support leads to long-term growth and competitive prices for consumers, or whether the regulatory regime is 'captured' by the incumbent producers. In Zambia, the incumbent firm has been able to maintain high domestic prices even though it is able to export sugar at lower prices. The incumbent has invested in expanded production, but there has apparently not been the same support for new entrants into the market, and high profit margins are therefore not competed away. While South Africa has not experienced the same growth, with other constraints (such as the availability of water), regulation has ensured relatively competitive prices.

There is therefore something of a contradiction in terms of the net effect of government influence on domestic sugar industries. While state support has certainly made it possible for increased investment to take place, as in the case of Zambia, it has also served to constrain the creation of more competitive markets. In terms of the region, this also means that there are few milling companies that are able to enter domestic industries, expand within those industries, and then compete within the region. In countries such as Kenya and Tanzania, the influence of the state as both shareholders in milling companies and regulators at the same time, has also affected the possibility of dynamic rivalry between firms.

Particularly in cases where firms are allowed to establish large operations and positions of market power, governments – through agencies such as sugar boards and competition authorities – need to ensure that firms do not manipulate special advantages to the detriment of consumers domestically and in the region. In Zambia, and to some extent Tanzania, firms have seemingly been able to leverage their market power to affect competitive outcomes along the entire value chain. In Tanzania, this has taken the form of exclusive arrangements with distributors.

Although beyond the scope of this study, it is also important to note that regional competition can also be constrained by structural bottlenecks such as poor road networks. Furthermore, if growers are not able to use new technologies to produce high-quality cane, then millers will not be able to compete domestically and in the region. The prevalence of cane poaching in Kenya is an example of ineffective enforcement of regulatory provisions that results in a constraint on the ability of millers in that country to compete effectively.

Conclusion

The realities of the sugar industry mean that efficient production requires growers typically to deliver sugar cane to the nearest mill, and for mills to have long-term relationships with growers to ensure their requirements are met in terms of volumes of cane and quality. There is thus a strong rationale for vertical coordination and not for competition among mills for sugar cane supply. This provides sugar mills with buyer power over cane growers in the short term. But, if the mills are opportunistic in exploiting this power then it will impact on the decisions of growers, thus undermining the efficiency of the whole supply chain. Vertical cane supply agreements entrench this relationship and limit competition among millers for sugar cane.

The market outcomes depend on whether there is competition between rival millers in the sale of refined sugar within countries and across the region. This depends on the degree of concentration, regulatory and other barriers to entry and expansion, and obstacles with regard to competition across countries. Some of the intrinsic barriers to entry, such as the sunk costs and the time required to establish a greenfield sugar business, as well as the costs to get the product to market, can be lessened by proactive government support. However, the record is of government intervention weighing more heavily on the side of protecting incumbents and supporting inefficient producers.

Large milling firms have been able to exert a degree of market power in some of the analysed markets. It has been observed that close relationships between these multinationals and governments have resulted in stable, non-competitive markets where these firms have been able to leverage the favourable regulatory environment to the benefit of their international shareholders.

The progressive liberalisation of global markets provides significant opportunities to grow the industry across southern and East Africa. This requires a reorientation of policies to support investment and competitive rivalry within a more integrated region. In order for the developmental benefits of increased regional integration and trade to be realised, policy-makers need to better harmonise their consideration of policies that affect the sugar industry. Specifically, they will need to better manage the nexus between the protection of domestic producers (industrial policy) and microeconomic considerations of the high prices faced by consumers in the short to medium term for food products such as sugar in particular.

While firms have strategically positioned themselves in markets that are characterised by trade and investment incentives, the competitive outcomes in the region are more likely to be affected by protectionism. Protectionist policies are not necessarily misplaced in the context of the distortions in international markets, but they can be severely undermined if the correct incentives (and support mechanisms) are not given to domestic firms to increase their competitiveness on the basis of innovation and increased efficiency. For instance, this could involve placing conditions on continued state protection that require firms to meet certain production or export targets. On the other hand, this could also involve the state addressing key bottlenecks such as the distortions in the supply of quality sugar cane by making the supply of key agricultural inputs more affordable and reliable. In this way, countries that have followed the strategy of increasing entry into the sugar industry (Kenya and Tanzania) can achieve the goal of inclusive growth and the development of local industry, while ensuring that there is dynamic rivalry within the domestic market.

Competition authorities and regulators have a role to play in terms of ensuring that firms that develop positions of market power or are afforded the protection to grow their capabilities are still prevented from abusing this market power to the detriment of consumers. Additionally, coordination between competition authorities within the region will help to limit the potential for firms to coordinate their strategies at a regional level by allocating geographic markets, for instance.

Notes

1 White sugar can be refined further to produce speciality sugars such as icing sugar, castor sugar, invert sugar, treacle sugar, liquid sugar and caramel.

2 The percentage for Zambia is an approximation based on the hectares of land under cane in the hands of out-growers as opposed to nucleus estates, and is not based on the source of sugar cane crushed at mills.

3 Note that the domestic consumption data for South Africa is for the SACU.

4 Malawi also has a significant sugar industry.

5 Estimates for South Africa, Tanzania and Zambia are based on the authors' calculations from available data on total cane crushed and sugar produced in 2011.

6 Source for Kenya is the Kenya Sugar Board (2011), and for Tanzania is authors' estimate from production data. Note that in Kenya there are significant differences between older and newer millers, with varying levels of efficiency.

7 South African Sugar Association (SASA) Sugar Industry Directory 2011/2012, taking hectares harvested for milling

8 Tanzania Sugar Growers Association (TASGA), 2013

9 Authors' estimates from interviews with firms

10 As reflected in the annual reports of the main producers

11 See http://www.illovosugar.co.za/UserContent/Documents/History-MilestonesBooklet.pdf

12 This was acquired in 1998 (see http://www.illovosugar.co.za/UserContent/Documents/History-MilestonesBooklet.pdf)

13 The fifth firm in the market is a new entrant, Manyara Sugar Company.

14 Unless otherwise indicated, information from http://www.illovosugar.co.za/UserContent/Documents/History-MilestonesBooklet.pdf

15 Illovo Sugar Ltd Integrated Report 2013, p55

16 Illovo Sugar Ltd Integrated Report 2013, p121

17 Tongaat Hulett Integrated annual report 2013/14, p82

18 Tongaat Hulett Integrated annual report 2013/14, p83

19 Tongaat Hulett estimated that establishing a 200 000-tonne greenfield operation including infrastructure, agricultural assets and sugar mill would cost around ZAR5–6 billion (integrated annual report 2013, p4).

20 Sugar Board of Tanzania. See http://www.sbt.go.tz/index.php/factories

21 See http://www.sbt.go.tz/index.php/production-data

22 This includes Swedish-based Bagamoyo Eco-energy Africa's investment to produce 130 000 tonnes of sugar. See http://www.tanzaniainvest.com/agriculture/tanzania-agriculture-news/1124-swedish-company-invests-usd-550-million-in-tanzania-sugar-ethanol-and-power-production. See also Southern Agricultural Growth Corridor of Tanzania (2012).

23 See Chisanga et al. 2014 and FAO 2014

24 Company annual reports

25 It appears that Africa, Malawi and Nigeria also fortify their sugar.

26 Ex-factory prices are the prices for a commodity at the factory gate, net of all discounts and rebates, often for bulk sales. This differs substantially from the retail prices, which include retailer mark-ups, smaller pack sizes and transport costs.

27 Note that these are average prices for the standard product; there may be different prices, such as for industrial sugar to large customers.

28 This estimate is based on the independent estimates of LMC International and data sourced from millers. It includes the major cost components for production, but does not include the costs of distribution and capital.

29 It is noted that Zambia Sugar subsequently contested this price with reference to industrial sugar prices even though it had provided original estimates that largely reflected household sugar prices.

30 Note that in some classifications of Zambian exports, the European exports are given as being to Mauritius. This reflects the ownership structure of Zambia Sugar and the sales of sugar within the wider group.

References

Chisanga B, Meyer FH, Winter-Nelson N & Sitko N (2014) *Does the current sugar market structure benefit consumers and sugarcane growers?* Indaba Agricultural Policy Research Institute Working Paper 89

COMESA (2012) *Draft Report of the Kenya Sugar Sector Safeguard Assessment Mission.* Lusaka, Mimeograph

European Commission (EC) (2013) *Evolution of the sugar imports in the European Union from LDC and ACP countries: Report from the Commission to the European Parliament and the Council.* Brussels, Belgium

FAO Statistics Division (FAOSTAT). Accessed February 2014. http://faostat.fao.org/site/339/default.aspx

Kenya Sugar Board (2009) *Kenya Sugar Board Strategic Plan 2009.* Mimeograph 2009

Kenya Sugar Board (2010) *Year book of sugar statistics.* Nairobi, Mimeograph

Kenya Sugar Board (2011) *Year book of sugar statistics.* Nairobi, Mimeograph

Lewis M (2013) *Sweet Nothings: The human cost of a British sugar giant avoiding taxes in Southern Africa.* ActionAid

LMC International & Overseas Development Institute (ODI) (2012) *The Impact of EU sugar policy reform on developing countries.* UK: DFID

LMC International (2006) *Action plan for the Zambian sugar industry.* In Ministry of Commerce, Trade and Industry: Zambia National Sugar Strategy. Revised first quarter 2010

Nyberg J (2011) Sugar International Market Profile, Background paper for the Competitive Commercial Agriculture in Sub-Saharan Africa (CCAA) Study. Accessed February 2014. http://web.worldbank.org/WBSITE/EXTERNAL/COUNTRIES/AFRICAEXT/0,,contentMDK:21730621~menuPK:4900969~pagePK:146736~piPK:146830~theSitePK:258644,00.html

Serlemistos A & Fusco H *Vitamin A fortification of sugar in Zambia 1998–2001.* MOST: The USAID Micronutrient Program

Southern Agricultural Growth Corridor of Tanzania (SAGCOT) (2012) SAGCOT investment partnership program opportunities for investors in the sugar sector

South Africa Sugar Association (SASA) *Sugar industry directory 2011/2012*
Southern African Development Community (SADC) (2009) *Guide to the SADC Protocol on Trade*
Sugar Board of Tanzania submissions (2011)
Sugar Board of Tanzania submissions (2013)
Tanzania Sugarcane Growers Association (TASGA) (2013) submissions
Tanzania Investment Corporation (TIC) (2010)
Tongaat Hulett Annual Report 2013/14

4 *Competition, agro-processing and regional development: The case of the poultry sector in South Africa, Botswana, Namibia and Zambia*

Ernest Bagopi, Emmanuel Chokwe, Pamela Halse, Josef Hausiku, Michael Humavindu, Wesley Kalapula and Simon Roberts

The commercial poultry industry involves agriculture and industrial development, and is also characterised by varying degrees of competition and competitiveness. Poultry is the single most important source of protein for people in southern Africa. Ongoing and rapid urbanisation and income growth in the region also contribute to the growth in demand for poultry. A substantial amount of the demand, however, has, been met by imports from outside the continent.

Despite being the single largest agro-processing sector in the region, the substantial and growing trade deficit – which is mainly due to the imbalance in supply and demand in South Africa – points to an industry that is not competitive at the regional level. As poultry production adds value to agricultural output and creates employment, the industry is able to make a major contribution to regional growth. There is also great potential in the region for increased agricultural production in countries such as Zambia.

Developing a poultry operation requires significant capital investment at different levels of the supply chain. The two main inputs to poultry meat production are feed and breeding stock. Animal feed is made from the agricultural production of maize, soya and other products, together with vitamins and supplements. Feed requires processing facilities such as for the crushing of soya beans and the milling of maize. Breeding operations produce parent stock and supply the day-old chicks for broiler production. Finally, the chickens have to be slaughtered, processed and supplied to retail outlets and the fast-food industry, which means investments in abattoirs and the cold chain for distribution.

A competitive industry thus requires coordination, where the different components of the supply chain are brought together. In reality, the challenge that coordination presents, coupled with scale economies at some levels, such as in breeding operations, leads to vertical relationships and concentration, which militate against competition. However, low levels of concentration imply supra-competitive mark-ups of prices at least at some levels of the supply chain, resulting in a weakening of overall competitiveness. In addition, independent firms operating at just one or two levels of the supply chain will rely on their rivals for their inputs and for access to markets.

This chapter draws on the study undertaken under the auspices of the African Competition Forum in 2012 and 2013 on competition and competitiveness along the supply chain across Botswana, Namibia, South Africa and Zambia. It is clear that many of the same firms operate across the different countries covered in the study. In addition, the growth of the industry has partly come about through the regional expansion of the existing large firms, especially the large investments in Zambia to expand production capacity. This means that competition-related issues in the poultry industry need to be understood at both regional and national levels.

It is clear that the poultry industry is oligopolistic in nature, with the large firms operating in a number of countries in the region. Competitive outcomes in the region are vital to ensure that the success of regional integration initiatives provide consumers with competitively priced poultry products. At the same time, countries must make tough decisions to balance competitive prices with the development of domestic poultry industries. There is a danger that government policies designed to protect and develop local production could decrease competition within a country and that the benefits from these policy interventions could be captured by the large firms and their shareholders.

While each of the four countries has adopted policies at different times to protect and develop its domestic poultry industry, the most important question is how a more dynamic and competitive poultry industry can be developed at the regional level – which involves higher levels of investment and job creation – to add value to agricultural production. While there is a temptation to support national champions that promise lower costs through large-scale operations, this risks undermining competition between the poultry producers and a more competitive industry overall. The study's findings suggest that firms in each country have been able to exert a degree of market power at certain levels of the value chain.

In light of the objectives of the book, this chapter analyses the dynamics of the poultry industry within the region, drawing on assessments of the industry in each country and from these building up a regional picture highlighting the interconnected issues of competition, regional integration, tariff and non-tariff barriers, transport infrastructure and policy interventions.

The next section provides the background and describes the nature of the industry. Thereafter, the development of poultry production across the four countries and the spread of the main producers are reviewed. Then, the competition outcomes, especially in terms of price at different levels of the supply chain, are assessed, whereafter what underlies these outcomes, including government policies and regulations, is examined. This is followed by the conclusion.

The nature of the poultry industry

Poultry production is essentially the combination of optimal genetic stock, in the form of breeds, with animal feed (see Figure 4.1). The upstream levels of the poultry supply chain are about the breeding stock. Poultry breeders are owners of the franchise rights or international licences to import great-grandparent and grandparent stock. The grandparent stock produces chicks, which are called parent stock. The parent stock in turn produces approximately 150 eggs per hen during an estimated 48-week period. These eggs are sent to a hatchery for incubation for about 21 days, for the production of day-old broiler chicks (commonly referred to simply as day-old chicks). The day-old broilers are reared for a period of between 32 and 42 days to a specified weight of between 1.6 kg and 2.2 kg, at which time they are slaughtered and processed.

Figure 4.1 *The broiler meat supply chain*

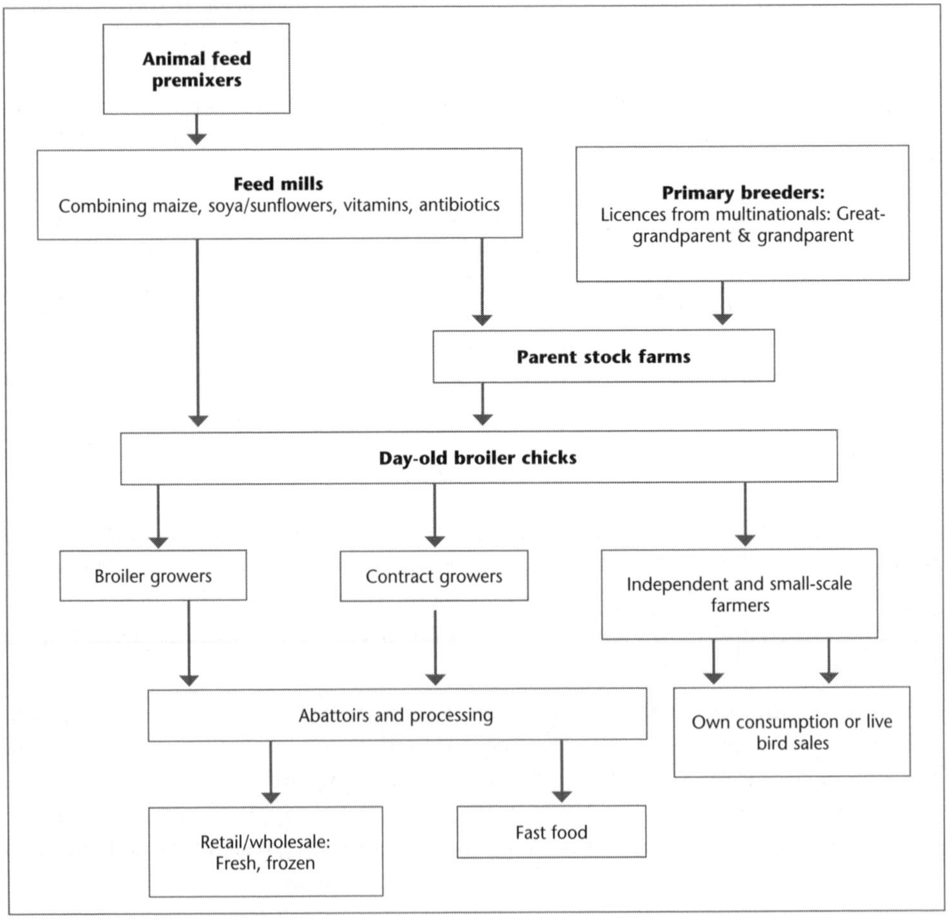

Source: South African Competition Commission, 2011

While the intellectual property rights are held by multinational corporations that undertake the primary research, the breeding operations can be undertaken locally at some point in the supply chain. Research can also be undertaken locally to adapt breeds to country conditions. In fact, two multinationals supply the breeds that account for the great majority of commercial poultry in southern Africa. The European-owned Aviagen Group supplies the Ross and Arbor Acres birds, while the US multinational Cobb Vantress Inc supplies the Cobb breed. Breeds accounting for a smaller share, such as Hybro and Hubbard, are also sourced from multinationals.

Producers seek high-performing breeds as measured by the number of day-old chicks produced per parent bird, the feed conversion ratio and the mortality ratio. The type of breed and its conversion ratio influence the time it takes for a broiler to reach the required size. The type of breed that is most suited for a particular country is influenced by that country's climate. While different breeds have been introduced, only a small number of breeds (two to three in each country, apart from Zambia where there are four) account for the majority of the region's production. While there is more than one type of Cobb bird, it is the most common breed (found in all four countries), followed by Ross, which is present in three of the countries, except Namibia. Large integrated poultry producers have their own farms and some of them also use contract growers to rear the broilers to the desired weight.

Feed is the major input into the production process. It accounts for between 50% and 70% of the total input costs, depending on the breed and conversion ratio. Feed is mainly comprised of a combination of maize and soya, along with small quantities of additional ingredients including vitamins. A broiler requires different types of feed at the various stages of its life cycle, which are mainly the pre-starter, starter, grower, finisher and post-finisher stages. As access to high-performing breeds is critical, the cost of feed is the main determinant of competitiveness for commercial poultry production. Not surprisingly, there are many links between the companies with the rights to the main breeds and those involved in large-scale feed supply.

Once the broilers are reared, whether by vertically integrated operations, contract growers or independent farmers, they are slaughtered and processed in abattoirs. Large abattoirs are industrial operations capable of rapid processing and packaging to suit different customers' requirements. This includes freezing, whether as popular individually quick-frozen (IQF) portions, or whole frozen birds. Some countries' consumers, such as those in Zambia, have a preference for buying live birds. The preference for buying live birds is typically the case in countries where urbanisation is limited or more recent. Only about 38% of the total production of broilers in Zambia is processed into frozen product. This is partly because the broiler market is characterised by many independent small-scale farmers who do not have access to abattoirs and processing facilities. Consumers in Botswana, Namibia and South Africa, on the other hand, buy mostly frozen poultry meat products. In Namibia and South Africa, between 80% and just over 90% of all poultry meat is sold frozen as either IQF or whole frozen birds.[1]

Barriers to entry and requirements for competitiveness

The large poultry producers operate at each level of the value chain. A firm wishing to enter and develop poultry operations on multiple levels of the value chain requires significant investment capital outlay. For example, the only large-scale producer in Namibia, Namib Poultry Industries (NPI), required an initial capital outlay of approximately N$600 million (US$73.17 million) for setting up its operations in 2012.[2] NPI is integrated at the parent, feed, broiler and abattoir levels and produced 250 000 broilers a week in 2013. In Zambia, Zambeef, through its partnership with Rainbow, announced a US$95 million project in 2013 to start an integrated poultry operation to place it as the leading producer in Zambia. The project, which became fully operational in 2015, has the capacity to produce 1 million day-old chicks per week.[3] This is associated with investments at other levels, such as slaughtering facilities.

However, a firm wishing to enter at only one level of the value chain (for example, as a broiler producer) will be dependent on the large poultry producers for access to the critical inputs (feed and day-old chicks) and slaughtering facilities. An entrant at the breeding (grandparent) level could struggle to access a suitable breed and would need a base of independent customers. There are only a few breeds available globally that are competitive and the large regional poultry producers own the rights to the recognised high-performing breeds. Running breeding operations also requires significant skill and experience. In addition, a new entrant requires sufficient capital for fixed investment and for working capital as it will take a minimum of one year from the delivery of grandparent day-old chicks to the first commercial-level day-old chicks. In Botswana, a hatchery with the capacity of 240 000 broiler day-old chicks a week was estimated to cost around BP40 million (US$5.26 million) in 2012.[4] To make such an investment, one must have confidence in buyers (that is, broiler growers) for the day-old chicks. The linked investments at the different levels of the supply chain are thus critical to the overall operation of the supply chain and the viability of the individual investments.

The grandparent level is driven by high volumes to achieve economies of scale. A new entrant's success will depend on access to sufficient customers and, ideally, an anchor customer. The most notable new breed in South Africa is Arbor Acres, which was introduced by the vertically integrated firm Country Bird Holdings (CBH) in 2007. In Zambia, Astral Foods, through its vertically integrated subsidiary Tiger Animal Feeds, introduced the Lohmann (Indian River) breed in 2009. It is worth noting that the introduction of these breeds (both sourced from Aviagen) was established by regional players that were able to link the breeding operations with downstream broiler production. As discussed below, even in the case of Arbor Acres, the breed's entry was delayed by exclusionary conduct on the part of another major South African producer, Astral. Indeed, these were cases of regional players introducing new breeds into geographic markets where the rivals' breeds were already well established, with CBH being the smaller party in South Africa and Astral being relatively smaller in Zambia. They are not therefore cases of greenfield entry by new competitors.

A new entrant at the feed level requires both access to the critical inputs (maize and soya) and the facilities to process them. A country's ability to produce or cost-effectively import these key inputs influences the likelihood of new entrants. The climate in Namibia and Botswana is not ideal for expansive maize and soya operations, so both countries depend on importing the crops, including in semi-processed forms such as oilcake. While South Africa does not currently produce large quantities of soya, production is growing and processing is being supported by the Industrial Development Corporation (IDC) and the Department of Trade and Industry (DTI). Nevertheless, the expanded production will not eliminate the substantial trade deficit such that prices will remain at import levels, with the main source being Argentina.

Zambia has greater potential for massively expanded agricultural production, which could lower relative prices in the region as a whole. However, the costs to the poultry producers also depend on the transport costs to the main sources of feed consumption, which in Botswana and Namibia are the poultry operations close to Gaborone and Windhoek, and in South Africa, those close to the Gauteng Province. As discussed below, Zambia started to export significant quantities of animal feed to neighbouring countries in 2013 and 2014, which lowered its poultry costs.

Feed operations can be established at a relatively small scale, but are driven by the firm's ability to source feed inputs. The mills themselves are often located close to broiler operations, which in turn are close to urban centres of demand. In South Africa, the largest concentration of poultry producers is in the KwaZulu-Natal midlands, which is between Durban and Johannesburg. This means it is well located for imports of feed constituents such as oilcake, while also being en route to the largest area of demand.

Poultry producers expanding operations into other countries tend to set up feed operations first, underlining the critical importance of this input. Astral, for example, has expanded into countries such as Mozambique and Zambia, by initially establishing feed production. It has subsequently established breeding operations in these countries.

Barriers to entry at the broiler level, however, are relatively low in terms of the capital investment required, and small-scale production is possible. Indeed, large producers often use contract growers to rear birds from day-old chicks. While various models exist, the most common model is for the contract growers to buy day-old chicks and feed from a large producer, and then sell the broilers back to the same producer once they reach the required weight. In effect, these broiler producers are vertically integrated with the larger producers' business. This points to potential entry barriers in terms of the ability to source day-old chicks along with feed, as well as the need to be able to process in order to have a saleable product.

Commercial abattoirs involve substantial investments and require large throughput volumes to make reasonable returns. An abattoir producing frozen poultry will require greater scale as it has additional costs such as spiral freezers, with industry estimates in

2012 putting the scale required at 500 000 birds per week and upwards.[5] For example, the Grain Field Chickens abattoir, established in South Africa in 2013, has a capacity of 800 000 broilers a week and cost around R130 million ($15.85 million) to build.[6] This is part of an integrated poultry business established by the VKB Group in the main maize-producing area of the country and linked with a soya oil press from which oilcake for animal feed is one product.[7] It also received substantial financial support from the government's IDC. Abattoirs that are not linked to large producers often battle to get sufficient volumes to make their operations efficient. This is evident from the closure of the DFC Abattoir in the Western Cape (South Africa), with the assets being acquired by Astral.[8]

Investments in expanded capacity are also influenced by the cost of capital and the ability to raise finance, with both being more challenging in Zambia than in the other countries. Given the large investments required, this further favours the established players and is motivation for the role of development finance, evident in the IDC's provision of finance for Grain Field Chickens in South Africa.

Each stage of the value chain requires a mix of skills: Upstream, breeders require scientific knowledge of the genetics and breeding operation; breeders and broiler farmers also require skilled veterinarians to prevent outbreaks of diseases; and abattoirs require skilled workers to ensure that operations function effectively.

Poultry producers also have to comply with various regulations at each level of the value chain. The regulations cover food safety, the environment, welfare and packaging. New entrants undergo lengthy environmental impact assessments and need proper biosecurity technology to control potential disease outbreaks. In addition, large retail chains also often have their own standards that producers have to meet if they are to sell to them.

The growth of commercial poultry and of the major vertically integrated producers across the region

While South Africa is the largest producer in the region – reflecting the overall size of its economy – the fastest growth has been recorded in Zambia, and this has been linked to major investments in new capacity. The requirements for being a competitive producer, outlined in the next section, mean that there are relatively few large producers operating across the countries, including through alliances and joint ventures with local producers. This means that the competition dynamics are both national and regional. Botswana and Namibia have responded to the challenges of developing their local industries by using protection to incentivise investments in local production. In Botswana, protection measures for the infant industry have supported producers that are integrated with regional players. In Namibia, however, the restriction of imports under the Import Export Control Act of 2004 has been to the benefit of a completely new entrant, Namib Poultry Industries, which was established by the Namib Mills Investments Group.[9]

Across the four countries, the largest two producers are Rainbow and Astral, both with their large operations in South Africa and expansions in Zambia (Figure 4.2). Country Bird Holdings (CBH) and Pioneer have the greater spread, given their associated businesses in Botswana as well as Zambia and South Africa. In addition to these four companies, there are also a number of smaller producers such as Hybrid and Panda Hill in Zambia, and Afgri in South Africa. After providing an overview of the trends in production at different levels of the supply chain, the expansion of the operations of the main companies is reviewed, after which the country-specific features are examined.

Figure 4.2 *Regional distribution of the major players, main production sites, 2013*

Sources: Company annual reports, various years

Growth of production across the four countries

Looking at the time frame of the study, which included data until 2012, South Africa was by far the largest producer, with an output of 1 billion broilers in 2012, compared with 25 million in Zambia and Botswana (Figure 4.3). Output in South Africa also continued to grow, relatively strongly from 2004 through to 2008, in line with the economy, and more slowly thereafter. By comparison, Zambian production almost trebled from 2009 to 2012, reflecting rapid urbanisation and growth in disposable income of the population, as well as the improved competitiveness of the local industry. Botswana's protection of its infant industry also supported very strong growth from 2010 onwards. Namibia started significant local poultry meat production in 2012 and has not reported significant growth since.

Figure 4.3 *Production of broilers*

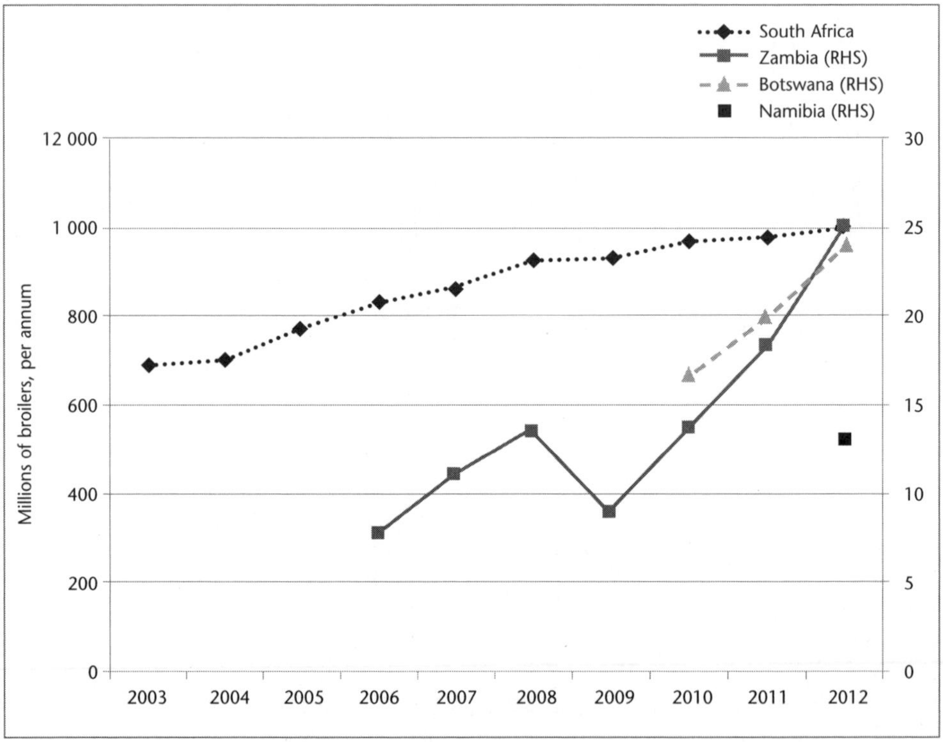

Source: South African Poultry Association, 2013;[10] Zambia and Botswana Ministries of Agriculture, 2013; Namibia data derived from the NPI, 2013

Interestingly, Zambia's production of day-old chicks is more than double that of grown broilers. This appears to be due to exports of day-old chicks to neighbouring countries such as the DRC, as well as broilers being reared in small-scale operations and sold live, and thus not being captured in the formal production data.

As might be expected, the data on feed production broadly reflect similar trends over the period studied. The notable difference is both the level and growth of feed production in Zambia (Figure 4.4). The massive increase in feed production in Zambia is associated with strong growth in agricultural production and processing activities leading to feed exports.[11] Zambia has had substantial growth in soya production and investments in crushing mills to produce vegetable oil, with the oilcake being used in feed. The country became self-sufficient in soya production, with exports beginning in 2013. Zambia also exports feed to neighbouring countries, with US$132 million of animal fodder exports in 2012 and US$81 million in 2013 after negligible quantities in previous years.[12] Most exports are to Zimbabwe, with South Africa, Botswana and Namibia also being significant markets.[13]

Figure 4.4 *Production of poultry feed*

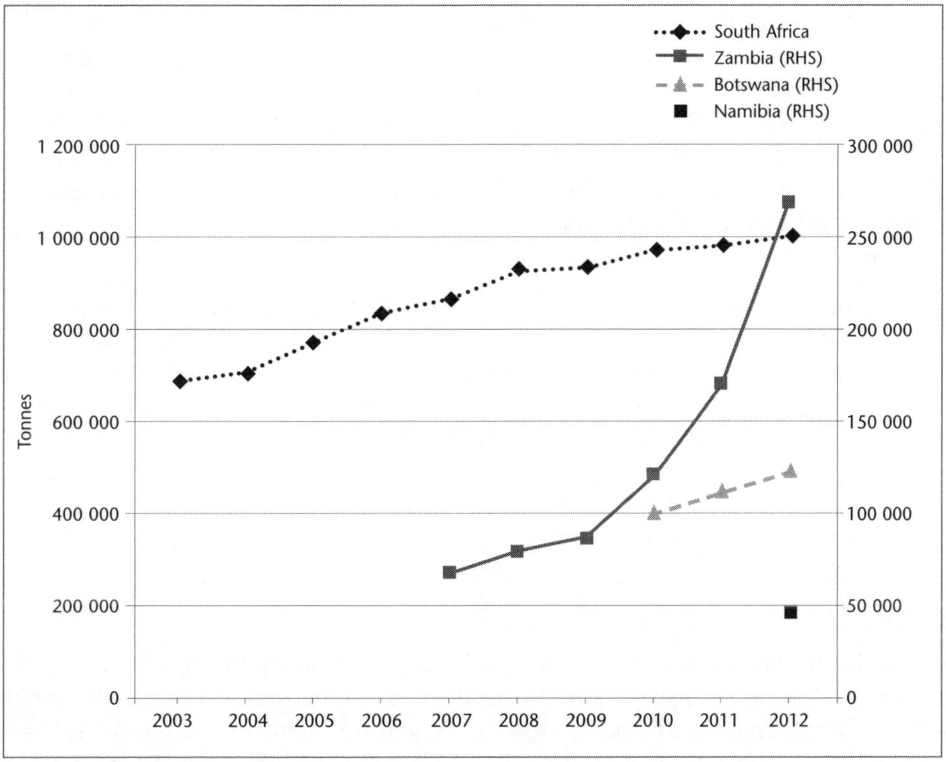

Source: Zambia,[14] Botswana Ministry of Agriculture and Namibia data derived from NPI, South Africa Animal Feed Manufacturers Association, 2013

The increase in feed production in South Africa between 2004 and 2008 ties in with the increase in demand for broilers, which then eased from 2008 to 2012. Botswana imports raw materials for its feed manufacturing mostly from South Africa, with a shift to Zambia in 2013 and 2014. Due to the increasing demand for poultry meat in

Zambia, companies are continuing to invest to expand their output. Poultry breeders in Zambia have been expanding their capacity. The major investments have been led by the large regional poultry producers, including in partnership with Zambian producers. An overview of the main companies in the region and their reach is the focus of the next section.

The main firms

Rainbow Chicken (RCL Foods)[15] *and Zam Chick*

Rainbow Chicken is the largest poultry producer in South Africa and has had very long-established, vertically integrated operations from breeding and feed through to poultry meat production. It is part of the Rupert family's Remgro conglomerate. It has the rights to the Cobb breed in South Africa, which it claims accounts for more than half the breeding stock in South Africa, and its feed operations are under the Epol brand. It has grown rapidly in recent years and has diversified its operations with the acquisition of the Foodcorp group and TSB Sugar in 2014, after which its name changed to RCL Foods. Total revenue of the Rainbow Chicken business segment was R8.1 million in 2013. In 2013, Rainbow acquired a 49% shareholding in Zam Chick, one of Zambia's largest poultry producers and part of the wider Zambeef group, which laid the basis for major investments in expanded production coming on-stream over the following two years.

The Zambeef group extends across the production, processing, distribution and retailing of beef, chicken, pork, milk, dairy products, eggs, edible oils, stock feed, and flour. It is also backward integrated from animal feeds into growing maize, soya beans and wheat, and forward integrated into retailing, including an agreement with the Shoprite supermarket chain for its butcheries in Zambia.[16] It has thus been one of the central players in growing animal feed and poultry production in Zambia. In 2013, Zambeef recorded turnover of US$300.4 million, with the poultry division jointly owned with Rainbow recording sales of poultry and eggs of US$30.0 million.[17]

Astral[18]

Astral is the largest integrated poultry producer in southern Africa. In South Africa, it has the exclusive rights to the Ross308 bird from Aviagen, substantial animal feed operations under Meadow Feeds, and downstream poultry production and processing operations with a number of established brand names. In 2013, it earned R6 billion revenue from poultry operations in South Africa and R4.9 billion from feed, with about half of the feed being supplied to third parties. In Zambia, it operates as Tiger Animal Feed and Tiger Chicks, with the Lohmann breed, also from Aviagen. It also operates integrated operations in Swaziland with National Chicks and in Mozambique, where it has a feed mill, hatchery and breeding operation.

Astral was originally part of the Tiger Brands food conglomerate before being spun off in the early 2000s to focus on poultry. It expanded into Zambia in 2010 with Tiger Chicks, a broiler breeding farm and hatchery. In a further sign of its internationalisation, it has alliances with Provimi, an international specialist in vitamins and mineral premixes for feed and Cargill, one of the largest global commodity traders.

Country Bird Holdings[19]

Country Bird Holdings (CBH) operates Supreme Poultry and Nutrifeed in South Africa, and Ross Africa and Master Farmer in other southern African countries. It holds the exclusive rights to the Ross308 bird in Africa outside of South Africa, and in South Africa to the Arbor Acres breed, both from Aviagen. CBH was founded by the owner of Ross Breeders Zimbabwe, (which subsequently merged with Crest and then with Consolidated Food Industries, listed in Zimbabwe), and Ross Zambia. CBH shook up the South African poultry industry with its rapid growth in the second half of the 2000s and its introduction of the Arbor Acres breed, challenging the two main incumbents. CBH has integrated operations in Zambia and Botswana, in each of which there have continued to be major investments and growth over the period. It is interesting that there is a major entrant into South Africa from a base in neighbouring countries, compared with Astral and Rainbow, which have expanded regionally from South Africa.

Pioneer/Bokomo/Brink

Pioneer Foods was built from the old Bokomo and Sasko cooperatives in South Africa, and still retains these names for different operations and brands within the group. It has diversified and has also developed operations and partnerships across the region, including in Botswana and Zambia, two of the countries covered in the study. Its poultry business did not perform well after 2010, with turnover of only R3 billion in 2013. In 2013, Pioneer sold its operations in the Western Cape to Astral and then exited poultry altogether, unbundling this as separately listed Quantum Foods.[20] In South Africa, its feed business is branded as Nova Feeds, while the poultry is under Tydstroom, and it has the Lohmann breed. In Zambia, it has been known as Bokomo (becoming Quantum Foods Zambia). In Botswana, it established Bokomo Botswana with PF Brink Ltd in the Bokomo Botswana business in October 2003, and has the rights to the Cobb bird.[21]

Hybrid

Hybrid Poultry was established in Zambia initially as a breeding operation and then an integrated poultry operation. It grew to be the largest Zambian poultry producer, with the rights to the Cobb500 bird in Zambia.[22] It is not listed and so data on turnover are not publicly available. It is reported to source feed from Zambeef/Novatek.

Country-specific developments

Botswana

The development of the Botswana poultry industry started in 1975, through the 'Thuo ya Dikoko' government programme, which involved the Ministry of Agriculture buying day-old pullets and then selling them to the farmers when they reached eight weeks. The project aimed to introduce poultry to small-scale farmers to increase the income of poorer families who did not own cattle. It also aimed to reduce imports. In the early 1980s, the government introduced policies to develop an import-substituting poultry industry, including a government-controlled marketing channel, the Financial Assistance Policy and quantitative import restrictions on the import of eggs and poultry meat into the country. The first two government policies collapsed and marketing was then dominated by large private sector firms. Quantitative restrictions on imports have been maintained under infant industry protection measures.

Botswana has continued to support local poultry producers with financial assistance through the Citizen Entrepreneurial Development Agency (CEDA) in the form of low-interest loans to small poultry producers. In an effort to build sustainable local poultry production, the Botswana government had financed about 245 broiler-growing farms by 2013. These small farmers engage with the large producers at the upstream levels of the value chain and sell their broilers to individual customers, supermarkets and government entities, and live birds to other large abattoirs. Abattoirs seek to integrate backwards to develop contract grower relationships with the smaller farmers. The abattoirs buy feed and stock on behalf of the small farmers. The small farmers are thus located in the supply chain between large firms supplying inputs and those operating abattoirs.

Namibia

Namibia effectively had no large-scale poultry production until the establishment of Namib Poultry Industries in 2012 under the infant industry protection provision. The impact of the support for a local poultry industry is that it created 650 direct jobs (of which 70% were held by Namibians in 2013). In addition, local traders who import and export poultry were estimated to employ about 900 people. In 2012, Namibia also had two other small-scale poultry operations, Zambezi Poultry and Naukluft Poultry.

South Africa

More poultry products are consumed annually in South Africa than all other animal-protein sources combined.[23] The poultry industry is South Africa's largest agricultural industry and is a major contributor towards agricultural GDP. In 2011, the poultry industry contributed an estimated 24 percent of agricultural income.[24]

It generated around R30 billion in local farm gate revenue.[25] The poultry industry as a whole has, on average, consumed approximately 30 per cent of the total maize consumption as the maize is used in poultry feed.[26]

The total number of direct employees in the broiler industry for 2012 was 48 118.[27] This includes those employed in hatcheries, rearing, processing and distribution. If related industries are taken into account, then the total amounted to 107 857 employees. This made it the largest source of employment in the agricultural sector.[28] Historically, two firms – Rainbow and Astral – have accounted for most production, with Country Bird growing in size since around 2006. Small- and medium-scale farmers do play a role as out-growers for the major producers and as independent operators, especially in rural communities. The South African Poultry Association (SAPA) classifies medium producers as those that slaughter between 120 000 and 250 000 birds per week. SAPA has 32 medium-size farmer members. The Department of Agriculture, Forestry and Fisheries estimates that there are about 2 264 developing farmers. SAPA established the Developing Poultry Farmers Organisation (DPFO) to assist SMME poultry farmers from previously disadvantaged communities to enter the mainstream agricultural economy. However, tough domestic conditions for poultry farmers have caused many developing farmers to exit the market.

Major challenges for SMMEs in the poultry industry are access to finance and access to markets. The government recognises the important role of small-scale farmers in rural development and has set up initiatives to assist developing farmers. However, rural farmers are often not successful in accessing these programmes. When rural farmers do access these programmes, they often lack critical skills, such as veterinary and husbandry skills. In some instances government projects are not economically viable. For example, some government-built abattoirs in rural areas have failed as they are expensive to run and lack the required economies of scale.

In a major development finance initiative, the IDC partnered with Vrystaat Koöperasie Beperk (VKB) to develop the poultry industry in the Free State Province in 2010.[29] The IDC owns a 23.9% stake and VKB the majority 76.1% stake in Grain Field Chickens. As part of the project, Grain Field Chickens buys day-old chicks from Eagle's Pride hatcheries and then sells them on to a group of 16 farmers. These farmers buy feed from the VKB mill. VKB has a 40% share in Free State Oils, which is a soya oil crusher plant. Grain Field Chickens has created nearly 400 permanent jobs.[30]

Zambia

The poultry industry is critical to Zambia's efforts to grow value-added agricultural production, create employment and reduce poverty among the population.[31] The industry employed an estimated 80 000 people in 2012,[32] of which 50 000 were permanent jobs and 30 000 were seasonal jobs.

The Zambian poultry industry supports other industries such as maize and soya farming, feed milling and transportation. These industries are all labour absorbing and contribute favourably to reducing youth unemployment as they do not require specialised skills.

The introduction of commercial poultry operations at the breeder level allows many small independent farmers a livelihood. These small-scale farmers purchase day-old chicks and feed from the larger breeders and feed manufacturers. They grow the broilers for their own consumption or they sell the broilers live, typically on an informal basis. With the country's favourable climatic conditions for maize and soya growing and poultry breeding, the potential for the development of the poultry industry and its contribution to poverty reduction is substantial.

Competition and outcomes: Pricing through the value chain

As poultry is the most important source of protein across the countries studied, the price of poultry is very important to consumers, especially to low-income consumers who spend a much larger proportion of their income on food. At the same time, the industry is a key source of demand for farmers and a substantial employer in its own right.

In this section, pricing at each level of the value chain is assessed. There is a particular focus on Zambia and South Africa, which are the largest producers and export animal feed to the other two countries. As noted above, Zambia in particular has the potential to assist the region in reducing or even eliminating the trade deficit. A country's competitiveness within the region and in relation to deep-sea imports is most influenced by the domestic cost of feed. In this regard, the prices of poultry in Botswana and Namibia are heavily influenced by their respective governments' policy interventions and protection policies. At the same time, both countries are also importers of feed, meaning that their underlying cost structure depends on their neighbours, as well as their ability to access deep-sea imports.

Feed

Poultry feed costs are largely driven by the cost of the two main inputs, soya and maize, with maize being the single largest component in terms of both volume and value (Grimbeek & Lekezwa 2013). Maize prices in South Africa have generally been at export prices, reflecting the substantial deep-sea exports that clear the market. This price is thus effectively the international price less the transport costs to get the product to those markets. The prices inland are therefore lower than at the coast. By contrast, Zambian maize prices have been supported by a government price floor, which has meant prices have been kept at relatively high levels. However, in 2011 and 2012, Zambian prices fell below those in South Africa, which is where they would be expected to be if there is large-scale maize production and net exports (Figure 4.5). In addition, the more competitive Zambian prices in recent years have also brought down relative prices in neighbouring countries such as Botswana.

Figure 4.5 *Maize (M) and Soya (S) prices*

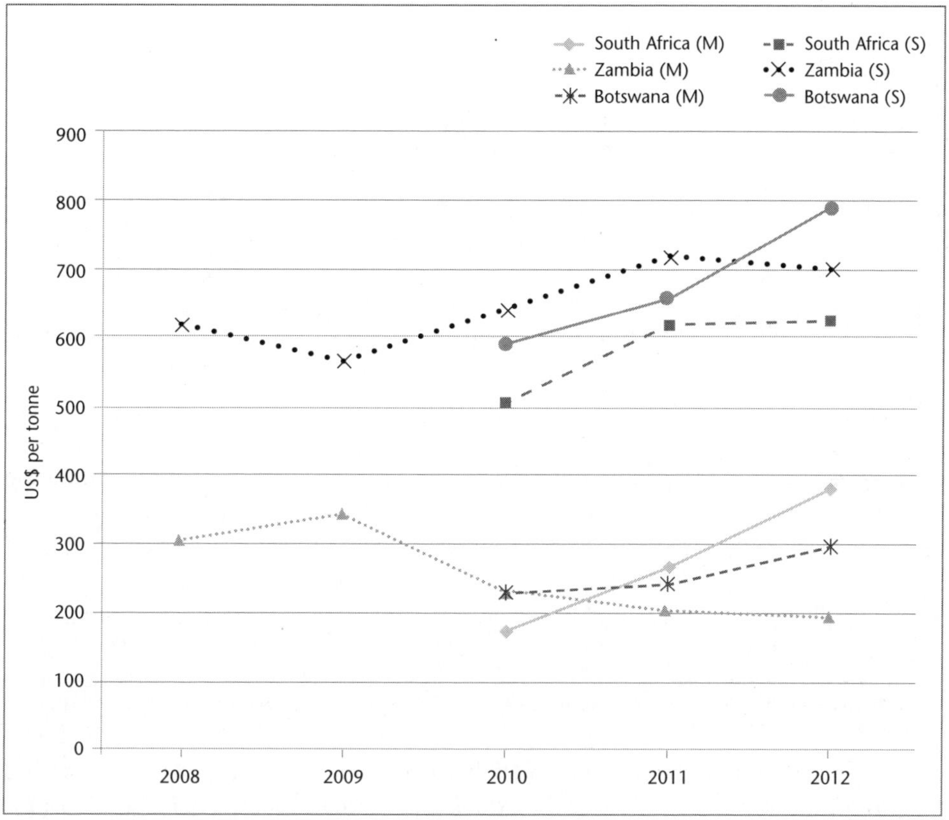

Source: South Africa SAFEX prices, Poultry Association of Zambia, and Botswana, 2013

By comparison, soya prices have been at import price levels across the region, although Zambia moved to become a net exporter to its neighbours in 2013. Prices in Zambia have been above those in South Africa, reflecting the prices being set by deep-sea imports and the greater overland transport costs required for imports to Zambia. As investment in soya production in Zambia started to bear fruit, the prices have come down to close to those in South Africa in 2014 and 2015 (Ncube & Zengeni 2016).

Considering how these key commodity prices translate into feed prices, the sharp increase in prices in Zambia in 2009 is surprising, while the fall in Zambian maize prices led to lower animal feed prices from 2009 to 2011 (see Figure 4.6). In 2011 and 2012, Zambian feed prices remained US$30–US$40/tonne above those in South Africa. Of course, large integrated poultry producers can source grain directly for their feed mills and do not have to rely on market prices. Instead, they set prices for independent broiler producers who have to purchase feed.

Figure 4.6 *Broiler feed prices*

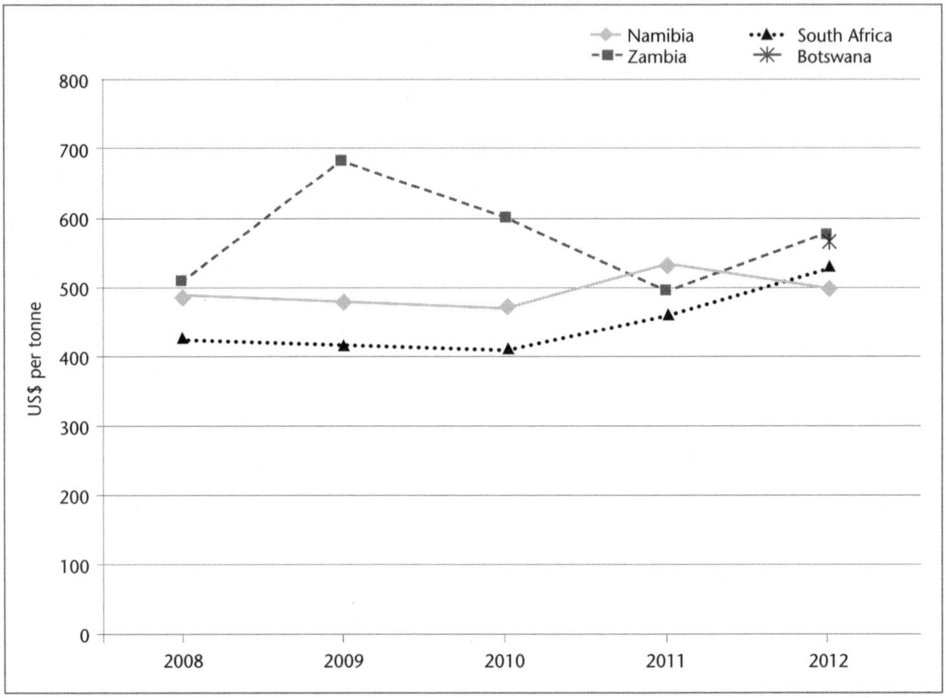

Source: Poultry Associations of South Africa, Poultry Association of Zambia, Botswana submissions by growers and abattoirs, Namibia data derived from NPI, 2013

The other main input, the day-old chick, has been much more expensive in Zambia than in other countries (and more than double the price in South Africa) (Table 4.1). Again, this is not the case for the integrated producers who have their own internal breeding operation. It is also somewhat surprising, due to the major growth in the Zambian poultry industry and the increasing exports of day-old chicks, and suggests market power has been exerted to raise the day-old chick prices.

Poultry meat

At first sight, South African producer prices have been far below those in the other countries, with a price per kilogram of frozen poultry being stable, at around US$1.65 over the period 2008 to 2012, while prices in Zambia climbed to around US$3/kg in 2011 and 2012, and prices in Namibia and Botswana were also substantially above South African prices (see Figure 4.7). This is misleading, however, because of the brine factor. South African products are brined, that is, injected with salt water. For most frozen poultry the brining is up to a proportion of 30%.[33] In Zambia, no brining is allowed, meaning that consumers are buying a kilogram of poultry meat rather than just 700 grams as in South Africa. Zambia also prohibits the importing of brined chicken.

Until 2012, Namibia relied largely on imported poultry from South Africa, which is brined at levels of about 30%. Local Namibian producers inject about 20% brine (the figure used to adjust the 2012 prices). In Botswana, brining is only done on a small scale. Botswana producers argue that their higher poultry production costs compared to South Africa are largely attributed to Botswana's lower quantities of brine.

The brine-adjusted prices are closer together, as the effective South African and Namibian prices are now higher when estimated per kilogram of frozen poultry meat (excluding brine). However, even with this substantial adjustment, prices in South Africa are still lower than in the other countries. While time series data are not available, prices in Botswana in 2012 were the highest of all (Figure 4.7), reflecting the impact of infant industry protection. More surprising though, given the trends in feed and grain prices observed above, is the fact that the Zambian prices have climbed even while feed prices were becoming more competitive. Zambian poultry prices in 2012 were some 40% higher than South African prices. The mark-up of estimated Namibian prices over South African prices, which was purely a result of the assumed transport costs, was apparently eliminated in 2012 with the start of local operations competing with imports.

Figure 4.7 *Broiler producer prices, per kilogram frozen poultry adjusted for brine*

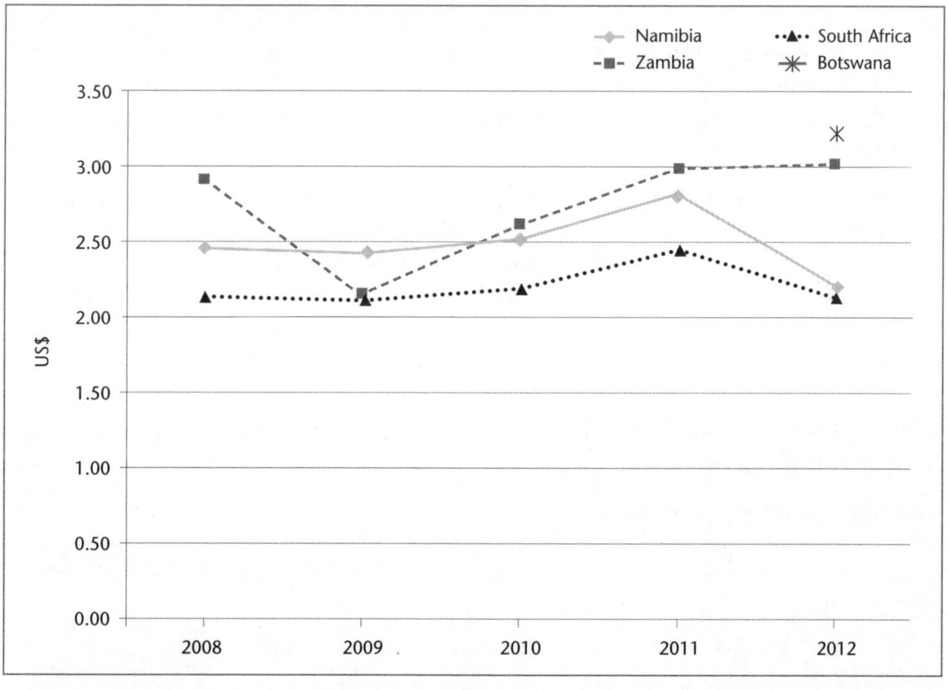

Source: Figures from Poultry Associations of South Africa and Zambia, 2013; Botswana submissions by growers and abattoirs; Namibia data derived from NPI adjusted for brine

Note: South African prices adjusted for 30% brining. Up until 2012, Namibia imported almost all of its commercial poultry meat products from South Africa and so the figures for 2008 to 2011 are the South African prices plus an estimated 15% to account for transport and storage costs. The 2012 number is an estimated producer price, correcting for 20% brining. While brining does take place in Botswana, its figure was not adjusted as it only occurs in small quantities.

The picture for Zambia is unusual, given that feed is the major contributor towards total production costs. Also, during the period under review, Zambia's production of both feed and broilers increased. Assuming that national demand did not outstrip the dramatic growth in supply, this could be indicative of the effect of considerable market power exercised by the largest producers on the market. Zambian producers also do not face the same level of competition from deep-sea imports as the South African producers do, and the local market is quite concentrated.

Producers in countries such as Zambia and Botswana can argue that other production costs are higher and that they do not have the same economies of scale, and that older and less efficient technology is used. In the following section, the cost and price build-up through the supply chain is evaluated more closely.

Cost structure

A cost build-up has been constructed for each of the four countries, which reflects the costs associated with the various levels of the supply chain (Table 4.1). This shows the differences in costs across the countries and potential areas of competitive advantages that may not be being realised due to poor competitiveness at other levels.[34] The figures were obtained by aggregating the figures from various producers and industry bodies, and then converting them to US dollars as a common currency. The starting point was the production costs per bird, and then the processing costs to yield one kilogram of frozen poultry as the IQF portions, which account for the majority of production.

It is clear that feed is the main cost in poultry meat production.[35] It accounts for about 70% of the total production cost of live chicken in South Africa, and just over 50% of the cost of a processed chicken. In Zambia, the feed cost is slightly higher, although because of other costs also being higher, feed accounts for around 60% of the live chicken cost. As expected, Namibia and Botswana's feed costs are higher still, given that the inputs to feed production are imported (and in Botswana there is a higher conversion ratio). Also, feed costs in Botswana could be driven higher due to the government regulation that requires 70% of feed requirements to be bought locally. This is discussed further below.

Table 4.1 *Cost build-up, US$, 2012*[36]

	Zambia	South Africa	Botswana	Namibia
Feed cost, kg	0.58	0.54	0.57	0.57
Conversion ratio	1.67	1.67	1.80	1.67
Size of bird	1.80	1.80	1.80*	1.80
Feed cost per broiler	1.74	1.61	1.85	2.00
Day-old chicks (DoC)	0.85	0.37	0.60	0.50
Other costs in broiler prod	0.25	0.24	0.53	0.30
*Live chicken (1.8 kg) cost	2.84	2.22	2.98	2.80

	Zambia	South Africa	Botswana	Namibia
*Live chicken (1.8 kg) price	3.90	2.64	3.39	2.84
Live chicken cost per kg	1.58	1.23	1.66	1.53
Abattoir cost / processing per kg	0.30	0.29	0.34	0.36
Processed chicken, per kg, cost	1.88	1.52	2.00	1.89
Processed chicken, per kg, producer price	3.01	1.64	3.15	2.23
Brining levels	0%	30%	Less than 5%	20%
Producer price, per kg adjusted for brining	3.01	2.13	3.15[37]	2.68
Processed chicken, per kg, retail price (frozen portions)[38]	3.20	2.93		3.66

*Botswana's poultry average weight is 1.65 kg. The figures have been converted to 1.8 kg for consistency.

The day-old chick cost contributed just 17% of the cost of a live bird in South Africa in 2012, with other costs accounting for approximately 11% of the total cost. By comparison, the day-old chick cost in the other three countries was substantially higher, with the price in Zambia standing out at more than double the South African price. The cost in Zambia accounts for about 30% of the live poultry cost and is the main reason for higher overall prices and costs. It is important to note that the day-old chick cost is the price charged to independent broiler producers, which could reflect the exertion of market power by breeders and not the actual breeding costs incurred by vertically integrated producers.

The higher cost for day-old chicks in Zambia, Botswana and Namibia could be attributed to the lack of economies of scale at the breeding level. Higher costs could also be attributed to government protection that regulates imports of day-old parent chicks in Zambia and broiler chicks in Botswana. However, Zambia is a net exporter of day-old chicks, which would appear to reflect low production costs. Given that by 2014 there were five breeding operations in Zambia, the cost of Zambian day-old chicks has declined with time as the market has become more competitive.[39] In Namibia's case, there is an additional expense for breeders as the grandparent day-old chicks are imported from South Africa. The breeding operations were also very new in 2012 and not yet at full capacity.

Abattoir and processing costs are quite similar for the four countries. In Zambia, it is therefore the feed and day-old chick prices that accounted for live chicken costs being 28% higher than in South Africa. However, the margin by which live chicken prices were higher in Zambia is even more, at 48%, which results in higher producer prices for processed chicken (see Figure 4.7). Viewed from another perspective, South African prices have been low, which might reflect external factors such as intense competition from deep-sea imports that the local industry has claimed were at dumped prices. This has been the subject of action by the South African government to impose duties on imports to support local producers.

Botswana's costs have been higher than the other three countries, consistent with higher producer prices. The mark-ups of chicken prices over costs were not as much as in Zambia. However, the price mark-up of the processed chicken producer over cost has been of a similar magnitude as in Zambia, albeit supported by infant industry protection in Botswana. The interplay of policies, competition and firm conduct in prices is analysed in the following section, drawing on insights from competition cases. The margins of the major producers over time are also considered.

Understanding outcomes: Competition, the conduct of firms, and regulation

The substantial investments and coordination along the supply chain mean that large firms are central to the poultry industry's development. This, coupled with the relatively small size of the markets in most countries, ensures that the industry is highly concentrated, and characterised by extensive vertical arrangements. There are inevitably competition concerns relating to whether the small number of producers compete vigorously and make investments in the expanded supply needed to meet growing regional demand, or whether the major firms dampen rivalry between themselves, within and across countries, and erect obstacles to smaller participants. Rather than advocating for a large number of competitors – which is not realistic, given the nature of the industry – the key concern is whether there is optimal competition: that is, dynamic rivalry among the small number of significant producers (Singh 2004).

Competition at the regional level

Competition operates at the regional as well as the national level. There is thus interaction between competitive outcomes and regional integration, such that consumers have competitively priced poultry products and firms make investments to realise the productive potential. Government policies have played an important role in protecting national industries and they have supported investments. In the short term, these policies reduce competition from imports and support the market power of the domestic supplier(s). In the medium term, if the policies are temporary, the investment in expanded supply can mean greater regional competition. However, there is a danger that government policies designed to protect and develop local production could decrease competition within a country and that the benefits from these policy interventions could be captured by the large firms and their shareholders.

Given the interaction between firms' decisions and competition at the local and regional levels, successful regional integration from a competition perspective requires close cooperation between the competition bodies of the different countries. For this to be effective, each member country also needs to develop its own effective competition law and implementation of the law (Fox 2012). The review of competition concerns across the four countries highlights issues of coordination and provides insights into the barriers to entry and expansion by smaller rivals.

The need for large-scale production: Significant mergers

The need for large-scale production is illustrated by the mergers and acquisitions examined by the South African Competition Commission, especially in the early part of the 2000s. The main poultry firms expanded horizontally and vertically in the value chain. Key examples were Astral's acquisition of National Chicks (Natchix) and Earlybird Farms in the early 2000s. Rainbow also expanded its operations through strategic acquisitions of Vector Logistics in 2004. Between 2010 and 2013, the tough climate for poultry producers, a strong currency (in the South African Rand) and competition from deep-sea imports from Brazil and Europe led to smaller producers being bought out. The main mergers were the Daybreak/Rossgro merger,[40] Astral/Corpclo,[41] Rainbow/Bushvalley Farms[42] and Pioneer/Darling.[43] Pioneer also effectively sold out its operations in the Western Cape Province to Astral.[44] The sector has stabilised subsequently due, in part, to anti-dumping duties being imposed.

The interplay between concentration and competition is emphasised by the pattern following the Astral acquisition of Natchix in 2002.[45] This merger led to Astral acquiring dominance in the supply of day-old broiler chicks to independent broiler producers.[46] This market power stemmed from the fact that Rainbow, the other large breeder at the time, produced day-old chicks largely for its own requirements and did not supply independent broiler producers. Following the merger, poultry meat prices increased and Astral's margins grew.[47] The merger had meant that Astral acquired effective sole control over the Elite breeding operation and enforced a provision which meant that CBH's South African operations, as a minority partner in Elite, had to source its day-old chicks from Elite.[48] This effectively blocked CBH from introducing a competing breed. Through contesting the arrangements on competition grounds, CBH did subsequently introduce a new breed, Arbor Acres, in mid-2007. This increased rivalry at the breeding level (including parent stock) filtered through to strengthen competition at the broiler level. The market shares and market power of the two big firms declined and CBH became a third major rival, along with smaller operations that were supported by greater competition at the breeding level (Grimbeek & Lekezwa 2013). Even with consolidation, however, the market was characterised by greater rivalry in 2014 and 2015, while, in response to deep-sea import competition, the South African government increased import tariffs in 2013 (Kwaramba & Tregenna 2014).

The Zambian Competition and Consumer Protection Commission approved the substantial merger of Rainbow and Zamchick (a subsidiary of Zambeef) in 2013. This shows the link between investment, achieving scale economies and more effective competitive rivalry. Zamchick operates at the levels of broiler processing and fast food outlets in the poultry sector. Through the joint venture in Zambia between Rainbow and Zambeef governing poultry, substantial investments are being made in breeding and feed operations. Given the high prices that have prevailed in

Zambia and that the two largest players in the industry, Hybrid and Ross Breeders (part of CBH group), collectively have had a market share of close to 75% for the production of day-old chicks, the investments in Zamchick provide a stronger rival.

In Botswana, there has also been a merger involving regional players as Ross Africa (part of the CBH group) increased its shareholding in 2012 in the dominant poultry feed manufacturer, Nutri-Feeds Botswana, from 60% to 100%, by buying out the stake of the Dada family. The share buy-back acquisition was approved with a condition that Ross Africa gets a local partner.

The South African Competition Commission has also investigated a number of instances of alleged collusion. The Commission initiated an investigation into possible price fixing against Rainbow, Astral, CBH and Afgri in 2009 and 2012. Pioneer and Astral subsequently admitted to cartel behaviour in the market for fresh chicken products in the Western and Eastern Cape.[49]

Industry associations

Botswana, South Africa and Zambia all have poultry associations where members develop common approaches to the industry challenges and lobby government. Namibia has an association of importers, which lobbies government against infant industry protection, while the sole local producer sits on the committee that determines import restrictions. Industry associations are potentially forums where competitors reach a common understanding on how to coordinate in their own interests rather than compete against each other. In South Africa, investigations have raised concerns about the exchange of commercially sensitive information between producers under the auspices of the association, which could serve to undermine competitive rivalry.

The Botswana Poultry Association (BPA) covers the whole supply chain aside from retailers. The secretariat rotates among members and representatives from the Ministry of Agriculture attend the meetings as well. Botswana also has a Poultry Liaison Committee, established in 2000. This committee comprises producers at different levels (day-old chick suppliers, broiler growers, poultry feed manufacturers) and retailers. The forum's secretariat is housed in the Ministry of Agriculture. Producers report information related to current poultry production volumes and retailers present information on the demand for poultry. If there is an anticipated supply shortfall, the committee will decide on the quantity of imports to be licensed. They will inform the ministry when to allow import permits and when the borders should be closed for imports. It therefore explicitly operates to restrict competition from imports.

Formed in 1904, the South African Poultry Association (SAPA) is one of the oldest agricultural organisations in South Africa.[50] The association represents all poultry producers and provides a collective voice to lobby government. It collects and compiles a wide range of statistics on the poultry industry. As discussed above, it has altered how it disseminates the statistics to satisfy the Commission's concerns about the exchange of information. The data are now more aggregated and the frequency with which the information is distributed to its members has been reduced. A separate Animal Feed Manufacturers Association (AFMA) represents the majority of feed manufacturers in South Africa, although given the overlap, a number of its members are also members of SAPA. It also collects a wide range of data and statistics on the feed industry and has adjusted how it disseminates information to prevent the exchanges that would be commercially sensitive and facilitate coordination.

The Poultry Association of Zambia's (PAZ) primary objective is policy advocacy and lobbying. Members share production and price information with PAZ, which then aggregates the information before distributing statistics to the members. This practice raises similar concerns to those identified by the South African Competition Commission.

Levels of competition in each country

South Africa

The increased intensity of competition in South Africa, with the entry of a substantial new breeding operation in 2007, is evident in the reduced margins of producers, after they had increased strongly from 2003 to 2007 (Figure 4.8). There are various factors that could explain the decline. During this period, there was an increase in domestic competition after CBH introduced a new breed, Arbor Acres, which, in turn, increased competition throughout the value chain. The South African poultry producers attributed their poor domestic performance and decreased margins to a steady flow of cheap imports. In addition, there were increasing input costs (maize feed prices) along with increases in electricity and transport prices.[51]

The falling profit margins in 2012 and 2013 have also been blamed on competition from deep-sea imports, exacerbated by a strong local currency in South Africa. In response to this, the domestic poultry industry called for increases in tariffs to provide protection for the industry that they argued is in decline. In 2012, the International Trade Administration Commission (ITAC) investigated South African poultry producers' claims that Brazilian poultry was being dumped in South Africa. It called for provisional anti-dumping measures (additional to the tariffs already in place) of 62.93% *ad valorem* on whole frozen poultry and 46.59% *ad valorem* on boneless cuts imported from Brazil.[52] However, this was a temporary measure.

SAPA, on behalf of its members, successfully applied to ITAC to increase import tariffs on frozen poultry in 2013. The import tariff on whole birds was increased from the previous 27% to 82% (the maximum bound rate under the WTO rules); carcasses from 27% to 31%; boneless cuts from 5% to 12%; offal from 27% to 30%; and bone-in portions from a specific duty of 220c/kg (roughly 17%) to an *ad valorem* duty of 37%. However, these tariffs do not apply to poultry being imported from the EU, as it can enter South Africa duty free.

The desire to develop poultry industries and with that, food security and job opportunities, has led to all four countries adopting policies to protect and support their local producers. While the policies may be required to incentivise investments in large-scale and competitive facilities, protection and support should be temporary. The protection limits competition, which could result in higher costs to the consumer in the short term. However, if these policies attract the desired investment in larger scale and improved productive capacity, this will lead to increased productivity. As is evident from above, while the rates of tariff protection in South Africa were increased in response to perceived distress in the local industry, the underlying causes of poor competitiveness need to be addressed, such as the cost of feed.

Figure 4.8 *Operating margins by company*

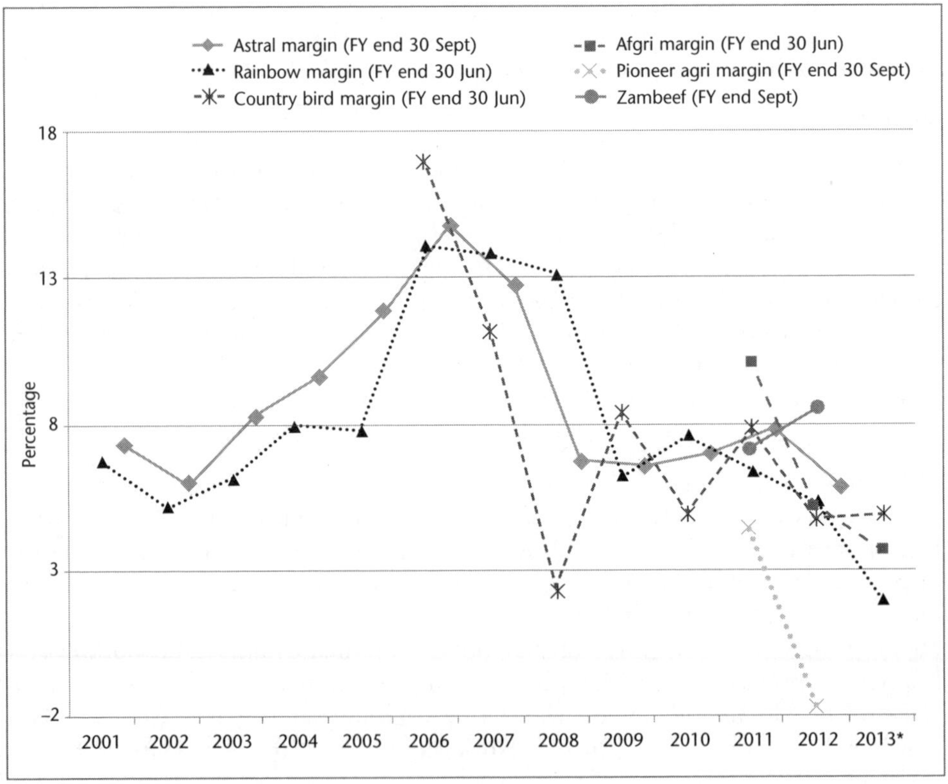

Source: Annual reports of listed companies, various years

Notes: 1 Margins calculated as operating profit as a percentage of total revenue.
2 Zambeef is a diversified operation that includes beef and soya farming.

Zambia

Zambian policies have been in line with a 10-year plan for the country's poultry meat industry, starting in 2005. The government and industry players projected demand both domestically and regionally for poultry and its input products. The government has sought ways to grow the domestic industry to meet the anticipated demand by protecting local producers and restricting importation of poultry inputs and final products. In Zambia, imports of poultry products are regulated and only allowed when there is a domestic shortage. The importation of poultry products, including day-old chicks, fertile eggs and feed is subject to stringent administrative procedures instituted by the Ministry of Agriculture and Cooperatives. Importers are required to apply for an import permit. The government maintains that it will continue controlling the importation of poultry products due to sanitary and phytosanitary considerations.

On the feed side, the maize farmers are supported, as there is a maize floor price set each year. This is likely to maintain the price above the level that would be obtained if there was no floor price, although, as illustrated in Figure 4.5, the maize price did fall relative to that in South Africa in 2010 to 2012. Importantly, the 10-year plan has substantially increased the capacity of the crushing industry for soya, which has been linked to major expansions in soya production. In 2013 and 2014, Zambia's soya production exceeded demand and it became a net exporter.

At the same time as growing local production, the protection means that prices depend on the intensity of local competition in Zambia, which has been limited with concerns about coordination among the few incumbents.

Botswana

Tight trade restrictions protect the dominant players in Botswana from import competition, notwithstanding the fact that the domestic producers all have strong links with regional groupings and, given the small local market, this substantially limits competition. Meat imports are subject to tight controls and a person entering Botswana is only allowed to bring in 5 kg of poultry products. Importing live birds and day-old broiler chicks is prohibited. The importation of fertilised eggs (to produce broiler day-old chicks) into Botswana is restricted. This means that the local breeders Cotoesloe (T/A Irvine's Botswana) and Ross Breeders have to expand their local breeding operations. Botswana also has a trade restriction on feed importation, with producers being required to source at least 70% of their feed locally. If there is a shortage of domestic supply to fulfil the 70% and the producer needs to import, it has to obtain an import permit. The price of poultry in Botswana has been among the highest in the region (see Table 4.1 above).

Namibia

In Namibia, there were no restrictions for poultry imports until around 2012/13, when the government implemented trade restrictions on specific poultry products to protect its infant industry against cheap imports. It used the Import and Export Control Act of 1994 to impose trade restrictions through a quota system to control the quantity of poultry meat products to be imported per month. The quantitative restriction on chicken meat imports came into effect in May 2013. This restriction is a temporary measure, given that Article 8 of the South African Customs Union (SACU) Agreement on Infant Industry Protection allows for an eight-year period. It was estimated in 2013 that the local supplier is able to supply 75% of the total demand and the remaining 25% is allowed to be imported after obtaining an import permit from the Import, Export and Trade Measures Office of the Ministry of Trade and Industry.

The possibility of granting infant industry protection to the poultry meat sector in Namibia attracted a lot of criticism as it amounted to protecting a single firm.[53] This could lead to abuse of market power if not effectively regulated. In this regard, the Namibian Competition Commission was tasked to conduct price surveillance in the poultry industry and to verify the industry's actual cost structures and production levels, monitor farm gate or ex-factory prices as well as to monitor regional industry developments. The higher price and levies are unlikely to attract other domestic producers as integrated operations are costly and the size of the market is not large enough to justify another large producer. Also, while the local producer creates employment, this must be weighed against those who were employed by importers.

The need for a regional view

It is clear from the above that there have been industrial policy concerns and competition questions in each country. What is missing are strategies to ensure the improved competitiveness in poultry production across southern Africa, to ensure that the benefits from agricultural production of the main components of feed flow through to lower costs of poultry production. This requires a regional view and increased regional integration, which ensures that agricultural potential in countries such as Zambia means improved competitiveness across the countries. A key question is how each country within the region can stimulate investment more broadly, while benefiting from regional trade with neighbouring countries where they have a comparative advantage. Feed and its components is the most important area as this is the largest determinant of production cost. South Africa has a substantial trade deficit in oil seeds, especially soya, even though it has increased its crushing capacity and local production. The imports have been largely from Argentina and Brazil and, given Zambia's agricultural potential, this represents a significant opportunity for increased intraregional trade if the investments are made to expand production and supply the same quality at competitive prices.

Transport costs

Action is required to reduce regional transport and related costs. To illustrate the impact of transport costs on regional trade, it was estimated in 2013 that the transport costs in Namibia accounted for about 20% of the total poultry production process costs. South African producers estimated that in 2012 it cost more to freight maize from Lusaka (Zambia) to Randfontein (close to Johannesburg in South Africa) than to freight it from Buenos Aires (Argentina) to Randfontein.[54] Based on the small volumes of Zambian feed exports to Zimbabwe in 2013, it was estimated to cost about US$90 a tonne to transport feed approximately 460 km from Lusaka (Zambia) to Harare (Zimbabwe). This is around 50% more than the cost of transport for the 600 km from the Durban port to Johannesburg. The distance from Lusaka to Johannesburg is some 1 550 km and means crossing two borders. The costs of this outweigh the sea freight costs from South America.[55]

Some South African producers indicated that they had, in the past, imported feed from Zambia. However, doing so came with challenges. Maize transported domestically in South Africa arrives in trains or on tipper trucks that allow for easy transfer into the factory. Maize from Zambia arrives in 50 kg bags, which requires additional labour costs to get the maize from the bags into the processing facility. In addition, to run competitive logistics requires reliable supply, which has not been the case in the past.

By comparison, transport costs for day-old chicks are relatively lower. This is because of the much greater value of day-old chicks and the fact that a day-old chick can be transported for up to 24 hours or a distance of about 1 500 km in specialised ventilated trucks and in some instances by air. For example, Zambian producers export day-old parent chicks to other countries in the region such as Tanzania, the DRC and Mozambique. Companies did not find border crossings themselves prohibitive when transporting day-old chicks. Rather, a bigger challenge relates to the reliability of the transport and delays that result in higher mortality rates.

Fully grown broilers are not generally transported for more than two and a half hours from the farm to the abattoir, as longer transport time results in weight loss and increased mortalities as the broilers become stressed. Once the broiler is processed, the fresh or frozen poultry product is transported in specialised refrigerated vehicles. The quality of the product relies on the cold chain remaining intact. The shelf life for fresh chicken is short, so producers try to get the product on the shelves as soon as possible and within 24 hours of slaughtering. This suggests why trade in chicken meat is, to a large extent, limited to frozen poultry.

The need for coordinated investments

Realising the potential within the region requires a series of linked investments in agricultural production, storage, processing and transport. Regional infrastructure and border crossings also need to be improved. Since 2012, there have been some improvements in regional transport (see Ncube et al. 2015). However, for substantial improvements, the region needs a coordinated regional strategy that will seek to break down barriers and harmonise standards (including sanitary/phytosanitary and brining) that will allow poultry products along the value chain to flow effectively.

Conclusion

The poultry sector is critical for a number of reasons. It is the main source of protein, especially for low-income households, and it also represents an important sector within the wider grouping of agricultural production and food processing. Growing commercial poultry requires linked investments in productive capacity from animal feed and breeding stock through to broiler production, slaughtering and refrigeration. Local production is therefore linked with multinational enterprises responsible for the main breeds, and industrial production is tied with agriculture in order to supply growing demand from urban areas. There needs to be coordination of large-scale investments at different vertical levels in the value chain (although not necessarily vertical integration).

The development of the industry depends on the decisions and behaviour of large enterprises, which, in turn, are influenced by economic policies and competitive rivalry. The study of the industry's development, pricing and costs across Botswana, Namibia, South Africa and Zambia has highlighted the challenges of ensuring both local investment and competitive outcomes. These are not necessarily in conflict. Without support for local productive capacity there cannot be competing firms in the first place. However, the concentrated nature of the sector due to the small market sizes, and the need for coordination through the supply chain, imply that firms may have substantial market power, whether unilaterally or through reaching a common understanding between producers. Such market power can be exerted to charge high prices that are not reflective of production costs. Where the market power exists in critical inputs, it further implies that smaller rivals can be blocked and the growth of the industry as a whole might be inhibited.

The data on production and prices shows that, while there has been rapid growth in Zambia and Botswana, and Namibia has established production in the form of greenfield entry, the prices of poultry meat have remained higher than in South Africa. The South African industry is not internationally competitive as reflected in a persistent trade deficit equivalent to around 15% of domestic demand, with imports largely from South America and Europe, even while the sector remains protected by tariffs. The prices of the key animal feed input have, however, become more competitive in Zambia, in line with agricultural production of soya and maize and investments in processing capacity. Despite substantial breeding operations and exports to neighbouring countries, the prices of day-old chicks in Zambia have been higher than in other countries. This suggests that a degree of market power has been exerted by the large poultry producers with breeding operations, which is consistent with substantially higher margins being earned in poultry meat production in Zambia than in other countries. By 2015, increased competition appear to have had an impact on day-old chick prices in Zambia. The margins on South African poultry production have been kept at relatively low levels by increased local competition, with the growth of smaller producers and competition enforcement efforts, as well as competition from imports.

The picture in Namibia and Botswana has been largely determined by policies to encourage local production to meet local demand. The support for the local industry has come at the cost of higher prices to consumers in the short term. In the medium term, the competitiveness of local producers depends on their being able to source feed cheaply, while the prices to consumers will also depend on competitive rivalry. This rivalry effectively works at a regional level and, in effect, three to four large poultry groups operate across all the countries.

It is thus crucial to understand competition and competitiveness at the regional level. The larger markets from integration could mean a greater degree of competitive rivalry and at the same time the greater level of investments required to grow the industry and compete with deep-sea imports. There are signs this has been happening. However, regional integration could exacerbate the tendency towards economic polarisation if not accompanied by appropriate regional development policies (Pratt & Diao 2008). The poultry meat industry is a good case in point. It would be short-sighted to argue that the countries in the study, as well as other South African Development Community (SADC) countries, should simply eliminate all trade restrictions. Doing so would be detrimental to the smaller countries' domestic industries. The South African poultry industry is large and well developed, and its existing scale economies would likely mean that South African poultry, along with imported Brazilian and EU poultry, would flood the smaller domestic markets.

This points to the important relationships between deeper and more balanced regional integration, and industrial policies. Indeed, in the medium term, the greatest potential for growth in poultry lies in countries where agricultural production underpins competitive animal feed supply, such as Zambia. This needs to be coupled with investments to achieve scale economies in productive capacity. The trade flows are the result of these linked investments in the context of imperfect competition (see, for example, Devarajan & Rodrik, 1989). In these circumstances, temporary protection could be justified to attract the necessary investment to support investment in local capacity. The large South African producers, seeking higher margins resulting from protectionist measures, have set up and grown operations in other countries in the region. However, long-term protection runs the risk of simply entrenching the market power of the large incumbents that capture the policy agenda and keep small players out. Careful oversight from competition bodies in the region will deter the abuse of protectionist measures.

In summary, the assessment here suggests that realising the benefits of deeper regional integration in the form of increased investment across countries, greater intraregional trade and more intense competition requires a number of steps. These include the following:

- First, standardising and harmonising poultry sector standards such as those relating to sanitary and phytosanitary measures and brining, coupled with efficient monitoring and testing systems at border entry points to effectively enforce compliance to the set standards and prevent disease outbreaks from spreading, while not inhibiting regional trade.
- Second, implementing phased reductions in protection between countries in the region. Some of the benefits that could be realised from relaxing protectionist policies include cheaper feed costs in countries like Botswana as well as greater price competition for end products, which would benefit end consumers.
- Third, designing effective policies to support the entry and growth of smaller producers, especially close to sources of demand in the smaller economies, need to be formulated. For example, access to finance, coupled with the high cost of capital in the region, hamper entry or expansion into the industry. Development agencies of individual countries and the World Bank[56] could play a greater role in facilitating access to finance across the countries in the study.
- Fourth, ensuring continued vigilance by competition authorities regarding exclusionary conduct and barriers to entry, together with greater cooperation between the authorities to guard against coordination and other anticompetitive practices across the region. This is part of a bigger trend where competition concerns increasingly have an international dimension as they affect more than one jurisdiction (Gal 2009).

Notes

1 Namibia Poultry Industries and South African Poultry Association Quarterly Broiler Price Report 2Q 2013

2 Namibia Poultry Industries communication

3 See http://www.thepoultrysite.com/poultrynews/30130/new-hatchery-planned-for-mpongwe/ The facility is valued overall at US$250 million.

4 Average exchange rate for 2012 at BWP7.61/U$1

5 Interviews with firms

6 'Start-ups take on big players and create rural jobs'. *Mail & Guardian*. Accessed August 2013, http://mg.co.za/article/2012-10-30-start-ups-take-on-big-players-and-create-rural-jobs

7 See http://www.vkb.co.za/index.php/en/2013-08-14-12-13-01/grain-field-chickens

8 See http://www.bdlive.co.za/business/retail/2014/03/28/astral-buys-darling-fresh-chickens-distressed-poultry-assets

9 With links to Dutch hatchery company Pas Reform with operations in South Africa, see http://www.worldpoultry.net/Breeders/Incubation/2014/12/Namib-Poultry-on-a-steep-learning-curve-1662433W/

10 The figures for South Africa are the number of broilers slaughtered.

11 A South African producer argued that the growth in Zambian feed has been driven by exports into Zimbabwe and the DRC.

12 UN Comtrade, retrieved from http://comtrade.un.org/

13 ITC TradeMap, retrieved from http://www.trademap.org/

14 Zambia figures represent the production of feed by the top five producers.

15 See http://issuu.com/rclfoodslimited/docs/2013_annual_report; see RCL Foods Ltd Investor presentation 28 August 2014, downloaded from www.rainbowchicken.co.za

16 See www.zambeefplc.com

17 See http://www.zambeefplc.com/annual_reports/

18 Astral Annual Integrated Report 2013

19 Country Bird Holdings (CBH) Integrated Annual Report 2013

20 See http://www.thepoultrysite.com/poultrynews/31987/broilers-for-astral-tight-focus-for-pioneer

21 See http://www.pioneerfoods.co.za/business-segments/international-footprint/; see http://www.bokomobotswana.co.bw/

22 See http://hybridpoultryfarm.com/

23 SAPA industry profile 2012, p17

24 SAPA industry profile 2012, p8

25 SAPA presentation to the Portfolio Committee on Agriculture, Forestry and Fisheries on 10 September 2013

26 SAPA industry profile, p9

27 South African Poultry Association (SAPA)

28 South African Poultry Association (SAPA)

29 See http://www.grainfieldchickens.co.za/index.php/about-us/overview-of-gfc

30 Value-adding in the Eastern Free State, *Farmers Weekly*, 31 January 2013

31 Poultry Association of Zambia, 2012

32 Poultry Association of Zambia, 2012

33 This is for IQF, which makes up about 60% of domestic consumption. SAPA annual report 2011 p8. The legislation governing whole frozen chicken allows for the carcass to pick up 8% water during production and for a further 4% brine to be injected into whole frozen chickens. The Department of Agriculture, Forestry and Fisheries was in the process of amending the regulations in 2012/13 to tighten brining practices, particularly for IQF portions.

34 The figures in the cost build-up are estimates based on discussions with domestic poultry producers and publicly available data. It is worth noting that these are estimates and are likely to vary, based on numerous factors such as seasonality where, for example, the price of feed could be affected. In addition, average conversion ratios were used. These ratios vary across companies and also for a single company over time as production methods alter.

35 The cost of fertilizer will impact the cost of feed. See Chapter 5 of this book for an analysis of competition in the trading of fertilizer.

36 Exchange rates: South African Rand and Namibian Dollar: R(N$)8.20; US$1; Botswana Pula BWP7.61: US$1; Zambian Kwacha: ZMK5147.30:$1

37 While Botswana producers do brine in small quantities, the figure for brining has not been adjusted as there is not clarity about the exact level of brining. Their producer price is still the highest (even without brining), compared to those figures adjusted for brine.

38 Note that there are no data for Botswana retail prices.

39 See Ncube and Zengeni (2016), who found that by 2015, the prices of Zambian day-old chicks were almost the same as in South Africa.

40 Competition Tribunal case no 57LMSep10

41 Competition Commission case no 2011Apr0016

42 Competition Commission case no 2011Nov0375

43 Competition Commission case no 2012Jul0370

44 See http://www.thepoultrysite.com/poultrynews/31987/broilers-for-astral-tight-focus-for-pioneer

45 See Ngwenya and Robb (2011) for a full assessment of the effects of the merger, and Grimbeek and Lekezwa (2013) for a review of developments in the South African poultry markets.

46 The Competition Tribunal had placed a condition on the merger, requiring the feed operations to be divested.

47 While Astral disputes the causality, it has admitted that the arrangements with the Elite joint venue, over which it acquired sole control in the merger, constituted an exclusionary abuse of dominance under 8(c) of the Competition Act in its settlement reached with the Competition Commission. Competition Commission Press release 'Competition Commission settles poultry case with Astral Operations' (www.compcom.co.za)

48 The requirement was that 90% of CBH's day-old chicks had to be sourced from Elite.

49 This matter formed part of the Commission's landmark R960 million (US$117.07 million) settlement with Pioneer on all outstanding cases in November 2010. The other cases related to Pioneer's activities in maize, wheat milling and baking. Astral reached a settlement with the Commission regarding coordination in poultry.

50 SAPA industry profile, 2012

51 CBH integrated annual report 2012

52 Provisional Payments on chicken meat from Brazil (ITAC press release), 13 February 2012. Accessed November 2012, www.itac.org.za

53 Discussion from public consultation workshop held by the Ministry of Trade and Industry in January 2013

54 According to interviews with South African producers

55 As reflected in Chapter 5, competitive transport rates between Johannesburg and Lusaka in 2014 had dropped to $110/t for bulk fertilizer, which appears low compared to the costs for feed from Lusaka to Harare cited here. The Johannesburg to Lusaka rates include taking advantage of backhaul opportunities from Zambia copper exports.

56 The World Bank (through the International Finance Corporation) has recently approved a loan to Country Bird to expand its operations in Zambia and Botswana.

References

Animal Feed Manufacturers Association (2012, 2013) *Chairman's report*

Country Bird Holdings (2012) *Integrated Annual Report*

Devarajan S & Rodrik D (1989) Trade liberalisation in developing countries: Do imperfect competition and scale economies matter? *American Economic Review: Papers and Proceedings* 79, 283–287

Fox E (2012) Competition, development and regional integration: In search of a competition law fit for developing countries. In J Drexl, M Bakhoum, E Fox, M Gal & D Gerber (Eds) *Competition policy and regional integration in developing countries.* Cheltenham, UK: Edward Elgar

Gal M (2009) Antitrust in a globalised economy: The unique enforcement challenges faced by small and developing jurisdictions. *Fordham International Law Journal* 33(1), 1–56

Government Gazette Notice No 5167 of 5 April 2013 on Restrictions of importation of Poultry products into Namibia: Import and Export Control Act No. 30 of 1994

Grimbeek S & Lekezwa B (2013) *The emergence of more vigorous competition and the importance of entry – Comparative insights from flour and poultry.* Centre for Competition, Regulation and Economic Development working paper 2013/1

Kwaramba M & Tregenna F (2014) International trade administration commission tariff investigations: An analysis of the poultry and paper investigations' *Journal of economic and financial sciences* 7: 619–640

Ncube P, Roberts S & Vilakazi T (2015) *Study of competition in the road freight sector in the SADC region – Case study of fertilizer transport and trading in Zambia, Tanzania and Malawi.* CCRED Working Paper 2015/3

Ncube P & Zengeni T (2016) The southern African poultry value chain: Regional development versus national imperatives. CCRED Working Paper (forthcoming)

Ngwenya A & Robb G (2011) Theory and practice in the use of merger remedies: Considering South African experience. *Journal of Economic and Financial Sciences* 4: 203–220

Pratt AN & Diao X (2008) Exploring growth linkages and market opportunities for agriculture in Southern Africa. *Journal of Economic Integration,* 29(3) 520–562

Singh A (2004) *Multi-lateral competition policy and economic development.* UNCTAD Series on Issues in Competition Law and Policy, United Nations: Geneva

South African Poultry Association (SAPA) (2012) *South African Poultry Industry Profile 2012*

List of interviews and additional sources

Interviews with representatives from each of the countries

Botswana
Bobbsie Chickens
Dikoko tsa Botswana
Feed Centre Botswana
Goodwill Chickens
Irvines Botswana
Ministry of Agriculture
Moleps Poultry
Nutri Feeds
Opti Feeds
Richmark Poultry
Ross Breeders Botswana
Tswana Pride

Namibia
Ministry of Trade and Industry
Namib Mills Investments
Namib Poultry Industry
Shoprite Namibia

South Africa
Afgri Ltd
Animal Feed Manufacturers Association
Association of Meat Importers and Exporters
Astral Foods Ltd
Country Bird Holdings
Pioneer foods
Rainbow Chicken
South African Poultry Association
Supreme Foods

Zambia

Bokomo (Zambia) Limited
Company Annual Reports and Financial Statements
Hybrid Poultry Farm Limited
Ministry of Agriculture and Cooperatives
Panda Hill Hatchery Limited
Poultry Association of Zambia
Progressive Poultry (tiger animal feeds) Limited
Ross Breeders (Zambia) Limited

Internet resources

Astral Foods opens Mozpintos hatchery in Mozambique. Accessed June 2013, http://www.astralfoods.co.za/MediaArticles_ArticlesView.aspx?FileNumber=454

Astral scrambles for bigger African nest egg. Accessed June 2013, http://finweek.com/2012/03/09/astral-scrambles-for-bigger-african-nest-egg/

Astral breaks ground in Standerton. Accessed June 2-13, http://www.astralfoods.co.za/pdfs/Press%20Release%20-%20Ground%20Breaking%20of%20Standerton%20Mill%20Press%20Release%20-%2026%20October%202012.pdf

Astral Voluntary Trading Update 30 January 2013. Accessed June 2013 http://www.astralfoods.co.za/PDFs/Press%20release%20-%20Astral%20Trading%20Update%20-%2030%20Jan%202013.pdf

South African Poultry Association Accessed on various occassions, www.sapoultry.co.za

Accessed April 2013, http://www.namibian.com.na/news-articles/national/full-story/archive/2013/april/article/swakops-chickens-ready-for-the-market/

Accessed April 2013, http://www.frontiermarketnetwork.com/article/1195-namibian-poultry-project-needs-funding-for-expansion

Accessed April 2013, http://sun.com.na/business/import-control-preferred-infant-protection.51672

Accessed April 2013, http://www.observer.com.na/business/1272-local-chicken-won-t-be-cheap

Value adding in the Eastern Free State. Accessed February 2013, http://www.farmersweekly.co.za/article.aspx?id=34977&h=Value-adding-in-the-eastern-Free-State

5 Regulation and rivalry in transport and supply in the fertilizer industry in Malawi, Tanzania and Zambia

Phumzile Ncube, Simon Roberts and Thando Vilakazi

Fertilizer is a key input for commercial agriculture.[1] However, there is generally low fertilizer usage in sub-Saharan Africa (AfricaFertilizer.org 2012: 5) and hardly any production of fertilizer in countries in southern and East Africa, aside from South Africa. Studies have emphasised the importance of transport costs in the price of fertilizer paid by the farmer, as well as the detrimental impact of a lack of competition in the trucking sector with regard to increasing prices (see, for example, Gregory & Bumb 2006). Many reviews over the years have considered the various reasons for the high costs of road freight in southern and East Africa, including regulations restricting participation and competition, the role of national and regional transport associations, inefficient borders and poor roads, and lobbying and rent-seeking by powerful local transport interests.[2]

The cost of fertilizer is largely determined by the costs of importing, including all the related transport and distribution costs, and the trader and agro-dealer margins. The scale and costs required for trading in fertilizer means that there are only a few major companies that control its supply in most African countries. This raises competition concerns. Together with transport and related costs, the intensity of competition will determine how much more a grain farmer in an African country pays for fertilizer than those in Europe or North America, where there are large fertilizer producers. Its importance and relatively high cost mean that fertilizer has been estimated to account for between 30% and 50% of the costs of grain and oilseed producers.[3]

Transport costs add substantially to the cost of fertilizer products, often accounting for 50% of the delivered price to farmers, when including all the related costs and margins. This is discussed further in the chapter.[4] Overland transport is obviously particularly important for landlocked countries such as Malawi and Zambia, while much of the best arable land in Tanzania is also located inland. The nature of competition in transport and fertilizer trading is potentially of great importance in determining the price to the farmer.

A number of African countries, including the three studied here, have implemented fertilizer subsidy programmes to support farmers in increasing their agricultural yields. These programmes have typically been targeted at small farmers on low incomes and who have benefited from substantial donor funding. In some countries, such as Tanzania, the subsidies were explicitly aimed at reducing the disadvantage faced by farmers located inland far from the import port, who otherwise paid much higher prices for fertilizer than those closer to the port in Dar es Salaam. Over the years, the subsidy programmes have grown both in terms of the magnitude of the subsidy and in terms of their reach.

This chapter is based on the findings of a study on competition in the SADC road freight sector carried out for the SADC Competition Committee. The main focus of the chapter is on the nature and extent of competition in road freight and between fertilizer traders responsible for importing and distributing fertilizer in Tanzania, Zambia and Malawi. The study considers the effects of regulatory arrangements governing transport on the fertilizer prices charged to farmers, as well as the impact of cost build-ups through the supply chains. In this context, it also reviews the effects of the fertilizer subsidy programmes in the different countries.

The chapter is structured as follows: The supply chain and the main firms involved in fertilizer trading are described; data on fertilizer prices and costs are examined; transport, trading and fertilizer supply are considered in more detail, including an assessment of the factors affecting road freight costs; a number of fertilizer subsidy programmes in operation are briefly reviewed; and then the conclusion is drawn.

The supply chain and the main firms involved

The fertilizer supply chain essentially comprises three main stages. The first stage is the purchase and shipping of fertilizer from a few major sources of supply, which vary with the type of fertilizer. Major exporting locations, which are also quoted as benchmark international prices, are the Black Sea (Eastern Europe such as the Ukraine port of Yuzhny), the Gulf of Mexico in the USA, and the Middle East. Nitrogenous fertilizer, which is the most important plant nutrient, typically is either in the form of urea or an ammonium nitrate compound. These require cheap energy to produce. Sasol and Omnia in South Africa both produce ammonium nitrate-based fertilizers from ammonia made by Sasol as part of its liquid fuels production, which uses coal and natural gas from Mozambique as feedstock. In this case the transport is from Secunda, located around 100 km from Johannesburg.

The second stage is the processing of the fertilizer at the port of entry, where it is transported from the port into warehouses and packaged into 50 kg bags, either at the port or in a bagging facility in the warehouse. Fertilizer can be imported already bagged, but shipping it in bulk form is cheaper.

At the third stage, the fertilizer is transported from warehouses to agro-dealers, possibly through depots and inland warehouses, and then sold to farmers. This almost always happens via road freight.

The scale required for organising cost-effective shipments together with financing means that a small number of international traders typically control the importation of fertilizer. These traders then supply the product through a local distribution network or sell on to local fertilizer distribution businesses.

It is important to note that traders may incorporate some of the transport, logistics and storage operations in-house or they may subcontract these services. Operating as an effective competitor at the trading level requires the ability to undertake this bundle of functions cost-effectively.

In Tanzania, fertilizer for farmers is imported through the only major port in the country, Dar es Salaam. This port is also used for transporting some fertilizer to Malawi and Zambia. However, most of the fertilizer for these two countries is shipped through Durban despite it being a longer overland distance. (The distance from Lusaka to Dar es Salaam is 1 951 km compared with 2 143 km to Durban and 1 048 km to Beira.)

This means that road transport costs from South Africa through Zimbabwe or Botswana to Zambia and Malawi are critical for ensuring access to fertilizer at competitive prices. While investment in upgrading the port of Beira in Mozambique meant some fertilizer being shipped through it in 2013 and 2014, to supply Malawi, the volumes were very small.

Transport and distribution: Road freight

The demand for road freight is closely linked to the performance of a country's economy as measured by economic growth and trade flows. Tanzania and Zambia have both recorded economic growth rates of 6% to 10% in most years since the mid-2000s, while Malawi has had much lower and more volatile economic growth. The southern and East African region as a whole saw rapidly increased volumes of trade in the decade from 2002 to 2012, almost all by road, because of the poor overall rail infrastructure. Perhaps the most significant feature of the trade data presented below is the growth of the DRC as a trade partner for both Zambia and Tanzania, in terms of both exports and imports (see Figure 5.1), albeit from a low base.

The high levels of economic growth in Tanzania and Zambia have been linked to an increase in the demand for the road transportation of goods, which is associated with substantial increases in regional trade flows. In Zambia, the growth in overall exports and demand for goods has attracted a large number of companies (including foreign firms) to the market and truckers make decisions on the rates they will charge on the basis of whether or not they will have a return load.

Figure 5.1 *Tanzania's merchandise exports to neighbouring countries, 1995–2012*

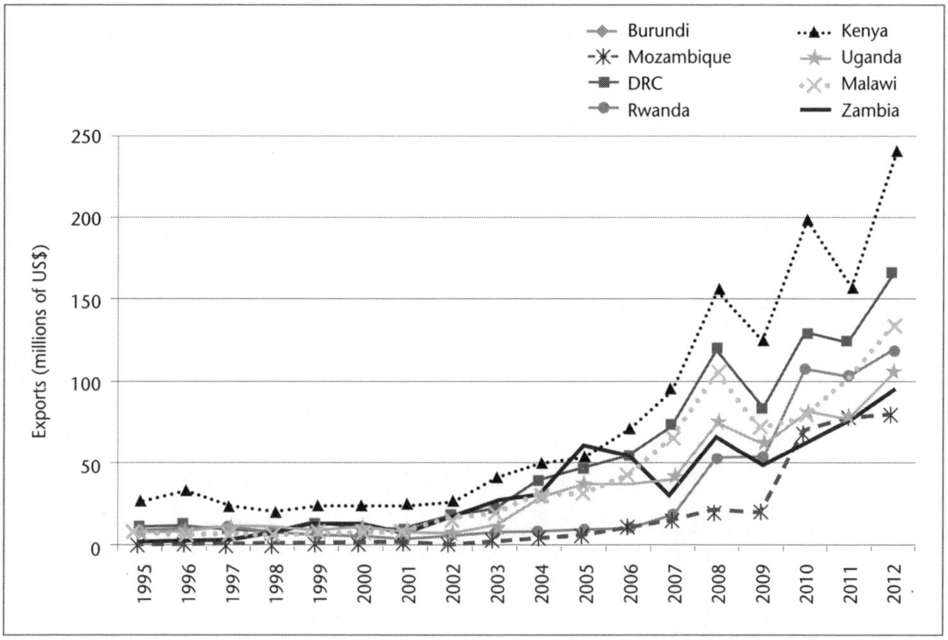

Source: UNCTAD, 2013

Tanzania has seen an increase in both imports and exports. Export figures show that demand for goods by neighbours has increased (see Figure 5.1), including for goods to transit through Tanzania (29% of port traffic in Dar es Salaam is bound for landlocked countries). Zambia is a major user of the Dar es Salaam port among land-linked countries as it contributes 47% to total transit traffic (Tanzania Ports Authority 2012: 32). The great majority of these exports are by road.

Zambia's trade increased dramatically over the 10 years from 2002, including with countries in the region. Most notably, the level of exports, particularly to neighbouring countries (such as the DRC), increased substantially in the period from 2005 to 2006 (see Figure 5.2). Increased trade has been driven primarily by the surge in exports to the DRC following the end of the civil war in that country, as well as the recovery in global copper demand and price, which affects the economies of both the DRC and Zambia.

While South Africa is not a direct neighbour, it has been the largest African export destination in most years. This is significant as it means greatly increased freight along the major route from the DRC and Zambia through Zimbabwe to and from South Africa (Johannesburg and Durban). Zambia also increased exports to Malawi and Zimbabwe after 2008, driven by increases in the exports of food items and manufactured goods. The growth in regional imports to Zambia has been mainly from South Africa, followed by large increases also from the DRC.

Figure 5.2 *Zambia's exports to neighbouring countries, 1995–2012*

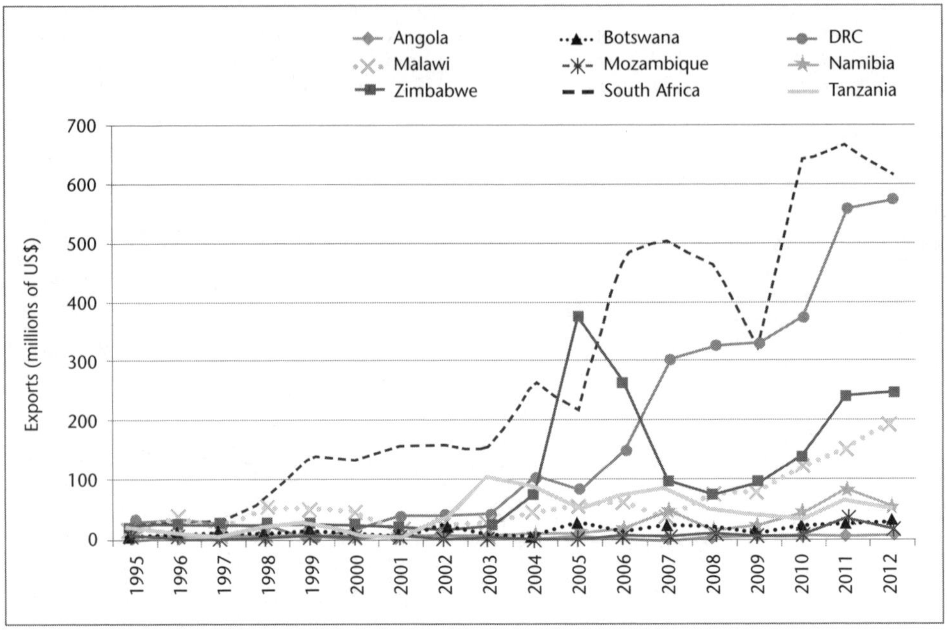

Source: UNCTAD, 2013

The sustained and very substantial increases in trade flows on the part of Tanzania and Zambia have had a major impact on the volume of road freight. This has been greatest along the routes to, and through, South Africa to Durban harbour. However, there have also been significant increases to Dar es Salaam, Beira and Nacala. Larger volumes of trade along these routes mean more efficient and larger-scale freight operations, and potentially more competition.

It is widely accepted that the price of road transportation in different regions in Africa is high relative to other regions in the world (Gregory & Bumb 2006; Raballand & Macchi 2008: 4; Teravaninthorn & Raballand 2009). While road transport is the main mode of freight in intra-African trade (UNCTAD 2009), the average price of transport in Africa represented 7.7% of total export value in 2012, which is twice the world average of 3.7% (UNCTAD 2013). These high costs have been assessed as significant contributing factors towards low agricultural productivity (Guo et al. 2009; Adamopoulos 2011) and as an obstacle to economic growth (Raballand & Macchi 2008).

There is an important distinction between transport prices and transport costs (Raballand & Macchi 2008). Transport costs can be defined as the costs that the transporter incurs when transporting cargo, whereas transport prices are the rates charged by a transport company or forwarder to the shipper or importer (Raballand & Macchi 2008: 2). In this regard, transport costs are not abnormally high in sub-

Saharan Africa, but transport prices are high on some corridors (Raballand & Macchi 2008). Several studies have tried to explain why the prices might be high compared to other regions in the world. One reason offered by Raballand and Macchi (2008: 3) is that official and unofficial market regulation and the structure of trucking services markets, especially in West and Central Africa, has contributed to very high prices. Similarly, Argent and Milanovic (2014) suggest that within the coastal countries of East Africa, for instance Tanzania, there are powerful trucking lobbies that seek to maintain control over the functions and rules governing the trucking industry.

One underlying reason for this rent-seeking behaviour is that it is a function of the small market size and limited alternative routes (see Arvis et al. 2010). Importers have low bargaining power in relation to powerful groups at ports and along transport routes to landlocked countries, and are also susceptible to rent-seeking within their own borders. In the case of fertilizer, the focus is on importers, among which are large multinational corporations. Along with governance and rent-seeking behaviour, Ward and Barreto (2011) found that high costs are driven by factors such as: industry structure and low levels of competition between service providers; low productivity in the trucking industry due to infrastructure constraints; and the regulation of regional and international trade in transport services.

The main firms in the importation, production and supply of fertilizer

While there appear to be large numbers of suppliers, when the main traders were examined the study found that fertilizer trading in the region consists of a small number of multinational importers that operate in more than one country, led by Yara and the Export Trading Group (ETG), along with a few significant domestic importers in each country. Yara (formerly Norsk Hydro), based in Norway, is one of the largest manufacturers and suppliers of fertilizer in the world. ETG was established in Kenya in 1967 and operates as a trader of agricultural commodities and inputs with operations across 30 African countries. It is vertically integrated into transport, including trucking, and has a logistics arm – PHL Africa – which transports fertilizer and agricultural produce. It has registered rapid growth over the past three years in Tanzania, Zambia, Malawi and Rwanda, partly due to the construction of a bulk blending plant in Zambia a bulk blending plant in Zambia.

In *Tanzania*, ETG and Yara are considered to be the largest importers in a fertilizer market of roughly 400 000 tonnes in 2013. Estimates of their market shares vary between 25% and 40% each, suggesting that their collective share has been around 60–70%. The higher estimates are shares of total nitrogenous fertilizer, which makes a difference in Tanzania as there is a local producer of phosphates, Minjingu. Other suppliers of nitrogenous imported fertilizer include STACO, with around 10% share, the state-owned Tanzania Fertilizer Company, and Premium Agro Chem.

The *Zambian* market has historically been dominated by Omnia and Nyiombo, with collective shares that have been estimated to be around 70–80% in 2009 in a fertilizer market of roughly 540 000 tonnes.[5] ETG and Greenbelt have grown strongly in recent years, while Nyiombo has lost a substantial share. According to one of the major fertilizer companies, estimated shares for commercial sales only (not subsidised sales) in 2013/14 were: Omnia 30%; Greenbelt 30%; ETG 10%; Nyiombo 7%; Zambian Fertilizers 6%; and others 17%.[6] There has also been an increase in smaller firms, including those set up by ex-employees of fertilizer companies. This may also be linked to the end of the cartel arrangements between Omnia and Nyiombo, which were found by the Competition and Consumer Protection Commission (CCPC) of Zambia to have rigged government contracts for fertilizer supply between 2007 and 2011.[7] [8]

After the judgment, the two firms were fined over US$20 million for their conduct, which was found to have largely affected the supply of fertilizer to farmers under the government's fertilizer subsidy programme, involving the allocation of geographic markets and price fixing. Omnia and Nyiombo have also been linked in various years to allegations of fraudulent relations with the government agents who are in charge of facilitating the tender process in the Zambian Public Procurement Authority and Ministry of Agriculture.[9]

In *Malawi* there have been a number of suppliers, with market positions changing according to the companies that have been awarded volumes under the subsidy programme. Agricultural Resources Ltd (ARL) is the sole distributor of Yara's products in Malawi. ETG has grown its share, and Omnia and Nyiombo both have a presence. The Malawi Fertilizer Company, part of the Farmers World Group, blends and supplies nitrogen, phosphorus and potassium (NPK) compounds.

Overall, the structure of the market at the level of fertilizer traders has an important impact on the outcomes at the road transportation level of the market. For instance, in cases where the fertilizer company is vertically integrated with a transport operation (as with ETG), it is able to internalise the margins typically earned by transport companies when the service is outsourced. On the other hand, when fertilizer companies outsource road transport services they can play a significant role in stimulating (or chilling) price competition between transport companies.

The pricing of fertilizer

Urea and calcium ammonium nitrate (CAN) were chosen for the study as good products to compare across the countries due to the availability of data and the wide usage of these products in each country. The pricing data reflect the national average prices in each country derived from monthly agro-dealer/retailer-level surveys.[10]

Three general observations can be made regarding average national prices of fertilizer across the countries: First, throughout the period, the prices of urea in the three countries were substantially above the benchmark international price, reflecting each country's position as an importer. Prices were at least US$200/tonne higher from May 2010 to mid-2011, and then more than US$400/tonne higher thereafter. While international prices decreased from mid-2011, prices in the countries studied continued to increase, meaning that the gap between international and national prices widened. One possible explanation for this could be that the costs of sea freight and insurance increased significantly during this period as well. However, the Baltic Freight Index, which tracks prices in international shipping costs over time, reflected decreasing costs from early 2010, albeit with some fluctuations.[11] Another explanation must therefore be sought.

Second, the increases in urea prices in Zambia and Malawi were greater in the first half of 2011, compared to increases in Tanzania at the end of that year. The same pattern is reflected in CAN prices (see Figure 5.3). This is consistent with higher transit costs, as Zambia and Malawi are both landlocked countries with relatively long overland transit distances from the ports. While international fuel prices did indeed increase by around one-third from early 2010 to early 2011, there are other possible explanations, including domestic factors in each country. These are explored in greater detail below.

Figure 5.3 *Urea monthly (national average delivered) prices, 2010–2014*

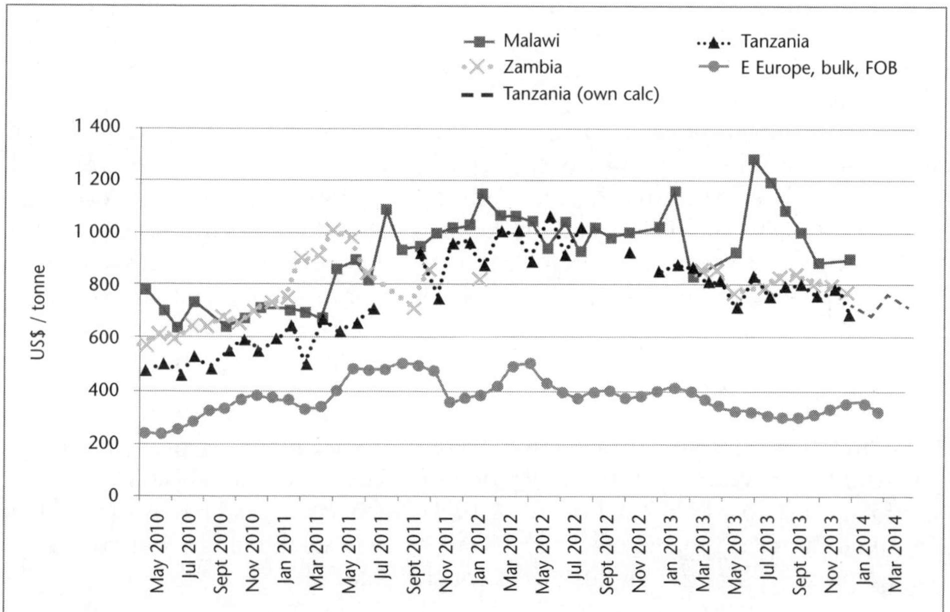

Source: www.amitsa.org, World Bank (MIDAS), 2014

Note: Outliers in the data where the value is different by more than 50% (absolute value) from the value in the previous or next month for which data is available have been removed. For example, Zambian urea prices showed an outlier of US$1 702/tonne in January 2012, and another outlier of US$1 619/tonne in June 2012, while Zambian CAN prices showed an outlier of US$1 477/tonne in January 2012, and another outlier of US$1 579/tonne in June 2012.

Figure 5.4 *CAN monthly prices, 2010–2014*

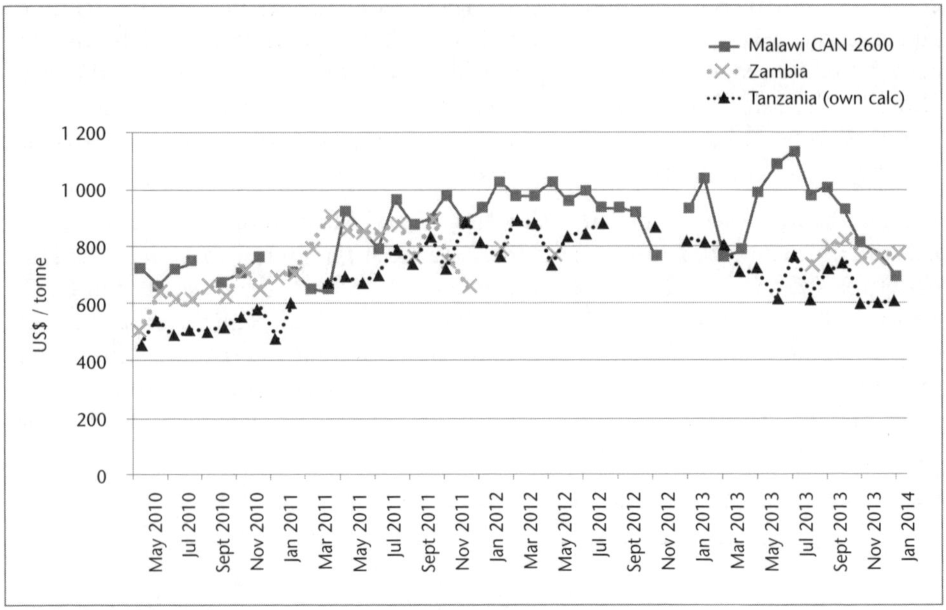

Source: www.amitsa.org, 2014

Third, the Zambian prices of both urea and CAN recorded a significant change relative to the other countries between 2010/11 and 2013. For both urea and CAN, the study revealed that Zambian prices in 2010 were in line with those of its landlocked neighbour, Malawi, and substantially above the prices in Tanzania, which has its own major port. However, in 2012 and 2013, the Zambian prices shifted to be in line with prices in Tanzania. This is in contrast to the expectation that prices would be higher in Zambia in a way that at least reflects the additional transport distance and thus the cost that is required to take fertilizer from the ports to the Zambian end user.

Table 5.1 shows a comparison of the average annual prices of urea across the countries for the years 2010 (from May) to 2013. The table also indicates the mark-ups (in italics) of prices in Zambia and Malawi over Tanzania, and the Black Sea FOB benchmark price (in square brackets). Given the very small number of data points, average prices for Zambia for 2012 were not calculated.

Table 5.1 *Average annual fertilizer (urea) prices and international FOB prices*

	Tanzania	Malawi	Zambia[12]	Average Black Sea FOB (Urea)
	516	696	635	
2010 (May–Dec)[13]		*+180*	*+119*	296
	[+220]	*[+407]*	*[+339]*	
	706	873	853	
2011		*+168*	*+147*	421
	[+285]	*[+452]*	*[+432]*	
	965	1 019		
2012		*+54*		405
	[+559]	*[+613]*		
	810	1 014	816	
2013		*+204*	*+6*	340
	[+470]	*[+674]*	*[+476]*	

Source: www.amitsa.org; www.africafertilizer.org; World Bank (MIDAS), 2014

Note: Slight discrepancies in the mark-ups calculated are due to rounding.

As illustrated above, the margin by which the average prices to farmers were above the international benchmark increased over the period. However, the prices in Malawi increased by much more than in Tanzania and Zambia. In the case of Zambia, one would expect prices to be higher than Tanzania because of the inland location. While this was the case in 2011, in 2013 the average price in Zambia was very close to that in Tanzania in 2013 (at just US$6/tonne difference) from margins of US$119/tonne over Tanzania in 2010 and US$147/tonne in 2011.

Assuming the FOB costs are the same for each country, (as well as handling and port costs), then the Tanzanian prices were relatively high. This could point to the costs of transportation within Tanzania and/or anticompetitive practices in the fertilizer market. The Malawian prices also appear very high, as the overland distances are similar to those in Zambia. Conversely, in Zambia, after increasing in 2011, in line with Tanzania and Malawi, prices dropped relative to its neighbours.

Factors that may have contributed to this include a number of important developments in Zambia, which have opened up the market to greater rivalry at the levels of both road transport and fertilizer trading. The comparison to the international benchmark suggests a combination of improvements in Zambia on the one hand, and a worsening situation in Tanzania and Malawi on the other, where prices increased substantially from 2011 to 2012 relative to international prices.

Another part of the price component of the study involved imputing competitive prices for urea in 2013 against which to assess the mark-ups in Tanzania and Malawi. To do this, the average delivered price for South Africa as a relatively competitive price in a country with a major port was used (see Table 5.2). For a landlocked country, the researchers added the transport rate from Johannesburg to Lusaka of US$110/tonne.[14] It is important to note that the South African price is an average price for sales to farmers across the country and hence already includes local delivery transport within South Africa. This calculation shows that average prices in Zambia were even lower than the competitive prices in 2013 by US$3/tonne, suggesting that the calculations are conservative and that the competitive benchmark should be lower by at least this amount (see Table 5.3). The exercise suggests that the prices in Tanzania were too high (by around US$100/tonne against the South Africa price) and prices in Malawi were too high by US$200/tonne.

Table 5.2 *Port and landlocked country price benchmarks, 2013*

Competitive port country fertilizer price	US$709 per tonne (South Africa)
Competitive transport rate	US$110 per tonne (Johannesburg to Lusaka)
Competitive landlocked fertilizer price	US$819 per tonne (Zambia)

Source: Author's calculations based on interview data and average pricing data, 2015

Table 5.3 *Mark-ups over benchmark competitive prices by country, 2013*

Country	Average fertilizer price (2013) (US$/tonne)	Mark-up over competitive price per tonne (US$/tonne)
Zambia	816	-3
Tanzania (compared to port country)	810	101
Malawi (compared to landlocked)	1014	195

Source: Author's calculations based on interview data and average pricing data, 2015

This confirms that there were substantial mark-ups in Tanzania and Malawi in particular, over what would be competitive rates in a 'similar' port and landlocked country, respectively. Effectively, the calculated mark-ups represent the portion of the difference between the costs of fertilizer in each country that is not (or should not be) accounted for by transport costs.

In order to understand what underlies the different mark-ups observed, the processes of fertilizer importation, trading and transportation at each level of the supply chain need to be analysed. The supply chain starts from sourcing the fertilizer and importing it, which for the countries examined here has essentially been only through the ports of Dar es Salaam or from South Africa (either through the port of Durban or from South African manufacturers). It is then necessary to understand the build-ups on the part of the traders all the way up to the pricing to the end customers.

Transport, trading and supply

Fertilizer arrives at the Dar es Salaam port, mostly in bulk. It must then be separated and packed into 50 kg bags that can be transported to importers' warehouses. This process can cause significant delays, often resulting in penalties to the importer, which are passed on to the clearing and forwarding company.[15] To expedite the handling of fertilizer, a private initiative was introduced by the Dar es Salaam Corridor Group (DCG) and the first vessel was discharged in 2004.[16] DCG's facilities, which are available just outside the port, are used to offload fertilizer ('break bulk'), facilitate clearance procedures, move the fertilizer out of the port area and bag the product for the importer. When the bagging of fertilizer was done by DCG, it could (in 2014) discharge about 3 000 tonnes per day compared to 1 500 tonnes by the port authority.[17] These facilities for breaking dry bulk have improved efficiency at the port. The fertilizer is then transported from the port to the warehouse, the cost of which is estimated to be approximately US$9–10/tonne.[18] Finally, the fertilizer is transported from the warehouse to the final user.

Costs and prices: A benchmarking exercise

The composition of fertilizer costs and prices was assessed for urea sold in Mbeya in Tanzania in early 2014, based on interviews with two fertilizer companies (Company A and Company B) operating in Tanzania and a study by the Tanzania Fertilizer Regulatory Authority (TFRA) (Ngowi 2013) (see Table 5.4). Mbeya is an agriculturally active region in south west Tanzania, 828 km from Dar es Salaam, where maize, rice and wheat are grown and fertilizer is in high demand. It is thus used as a benchmark for inland pricing.

Table 5.4 *Fertilizer price composition in Mbeya, US$/tonne*

	Fertilizer Company A Q1 2014	Fertilizer Company B Q1 2014	Tanzania Fertilizer Regulatory Authority (2013)	Benchmark	
FOB	**352**	**350**	–	**350**	
CIF	**402**	**400**	**420**	**400**	
Port charges	50	50	60	50	**+130**
Bags, bagging and storage	18.15	–	20	20	
Importer margin	20	–	–	10	
Sub-total: Ex-port warehouse (bagged)	***490.15***	***450***	***500***	***480***	
Inland transport costs	43	60	50	50	
Wholesale price	**573**	**545**	**563**	**560**	**+160**
Final retail price	**646.6**	**545**	**688**	**640**	
Chimala average retail list price (AMITSA)	**882**[19]	**882**	**757**	**882**	
National average retail list price (AMITSA)	**720**	**720**	**810**	**720**	

Source: Interview data from fertilizer companies; Ngowi, 2013

Note: Some of the figures do not necessarily add up to the total retail price in this table, due to the unavailability of estimates for some of the components. Mbeya is 828 km from Dar es Salaam.

Not surprisingly, as Table 5.4 shows, the estimates of the FOB prices from the two fertilizer companies and the TFRA are almost identical, as countries are price takers in an international market. Sea freight and other related costs are around US$50/tonne, while port charges and bagging add further costs of around US$50/tonne and US$20/tonne, respectively. Together, all these costs from the import source (on a FOB basis) through the bagged product in a warehouse ready for local delivery adds around US$130/tonne, including a modest allowance for a margin for the importer (not included by Fertilizer Company B, which also does its own bagging).[20] The TFRA data are for 2013, when there appears to have been slightly higher international prices, although the cost, insurance and freight (CIF) estimated price may also include a TFRA margin.

By comparison, the local transport and trading activities add around US$160/tonne to get to a final (net) retail price of around US$640/tonne at the fertilizer trader (see Table 5.4). Note that the transport cost is just US$50/tonne, and is even lower on some estimates (such as from Fertilizer Company A), while Fertilizer Company B has its own trucking operation on which it can include an internal margin. This means that an additional US$110 is included in the trader and retailer costs and margin over and above the transport cost ex-warehouse to the agro-dealer. The average retail list prices of the agro-dealer are substantially higher than this, based on the prices recorded at a town that is approximately 74 km from Mbeya, and on the average recorded at agro-dealers across the country including those close to Dar es Salaam.

The identification of around US$110 in excess charges in the price is also consistent with the very competitive final retail price of Fertilizer Company B in 2014. Key developments appear to have led to the opening up of the market, allowing more competitive offerings. These include the improved access to the port enabling a more contestable market. In effect, the developments in early 2014 are consistent with the assessment of the mark-ups between 2011 and 2013 for Tanzania. In addition, the difference between Fertilizer Company B's final retail price in 2014 and the FOB price – US$195/tonne – is close to the difference in 2010 of US$220/tonne for Tanzania overall, while for 2013 it was around US$350/tonne (based on the TFRA study) and US$470/tonne from Table 5.1, although the average retail prices are list prices and some discounting may take place. This is some US$150/tonne to US$250/tonne higher than the cost build-up suggests should be a competitive price. This accords with the study's assessment of the amount by which Tanzanian prices were marked up from 2011 to 2013.

These are significant differences and suggest that fertilizer prices in Tanzania are far above what farmers should be paying and that farmers there could benefit from more competitive rivalry.

The margin by which prices were found to have been too high is split between inefficiencies, regulatory issues, trader margins, and other rents that may be due to competition issues related to barriers to entry and the level of contestability of the market.

While interviews with individual firms were not held in Malawi, the mark-ups there appear to be even higher. Part of the explanation for this is associated with higher costs related to transport and storage, as regulatory restrictions inhibit competition and benefit firms that apparently have the necessary approvals. This is discussed further below.

The trucking industry in Zambia, Tanzania and Malawi

For both Zambia and Tanzania, there has been a sharp increase in the number of trucks and truck operators in the country, while transporters in Malawi remained relatively constrained by regulatory barriers among other factors. For example, in Tanzania between 2009 and 2013, the number of licences issued for goods service vehicles almost doubled.[21] In Zambia, the number of trucks increased following the removal of import duties on second-hand trucks in 2008/9.[22] Similarly, the number of trucks in Tanzania increased after the removal of surcharges on imports of trucks that are over 10 years old.

The road freight sector is also affected by the regulatory environment. The road freight industry – like any other industry providing trade services – is governed by domestic, regional and international regulations. These regulations work to enhance or to impede competition and market access in some cases.

Each of the countries in the study applies a separate domestic regulation for road transport services. In Tanzania, the Road Traffic Act of 1973 regulates vehicle mass on the roads and stipulates fees to be charged for overloading, for example. There is also the Surface and Marine Transport Regulatory Authority Act of 2001, which gives effect to the Surface and Marine Transport and Regulatory Authority (SUMATRA). This authority is responsible for licensing trucks, dealing with consumer complaints, and promoting the interests of the trucking industry generally.

In Zambia, road transportation is governed by the Road Traffic Act of 2002, which contains specific provisions pertaining to the issuing of road service licences or permits. Some of the quantitative restrictions for obtaining a road transport operator licence under the Zambian licencing regime were problematic, as they directly restricted competitive rivalry (Meeuws 2004).

It appears that increased volumes arising from the boom in trade have led to greater competition and falling trucking rates along major routes. Where these volumes are associated with, for example, copper exports to major ports, there are further possibilities for backhaul of goods such as fertilizer being transported in the opposite direction. Another reason for the increase in the number of trucks in Tanzania is the relaxation of government controls, which previously required that heavy loads be transported via rail.[23]

Working against seamless and lower-cost trucking is the fact that regulations inhibiting cross-border trade in transport services continue to be implemented

(Ward & Barreto 2011: 13). Important regulations widely applied in SADC relate to cabotage, which prohibits foreign firms from transporting cargo between two points within a foreign country, and the third-country rule, which prohibits an operator from transporting goods from another country to a third without passing through its own country of origin. The rule against cabotage has been highlighted in previous studies as an important determinant of competitive outcomes in domestic road transport markets insofar as it affects the ability of foreign registered trucking companies to compete in another country's domestic market. However, the impact of these rules has been disputed. For example, in relation to Rwanda, Argent and Milanovic (2014) argued that removing the cabotage regulation would not improve the competitive position of Rwanda's industry.

In the case of *Zambia*, the introduction of a single permit system between Zambia, Zimbabwe and South Africa in the early 2000s made a significant difference (Meeuws 2004). This meant that Zimbabwean and South African trucking companies could operate along the corridors alongside Zambian companies such that Zambian truckers held only around a 40% market share on the main corridors, even while restrictions on cabotage and the third-country rule remained (Raballand et al. 2007). The influx of competition from regional trucking companies into the Zambian market has, over time, reduced transport costs to be on par with costs in South Africa. In effect, the main companies could run operations across the countries with trucks registered in each, so lifting cabotage and third-country rules would probably have only a muted effect.

In the Zambian market, the copper mines appear also to have good bargaining power. The rates obtained by the mines in 2013/14 averaged US$116/tonne from the Copperbelt to Johannesburg, or around US$0.06/tonne/km.[24] The rates from Durban and Johannesburg to Lusaka were somewhat higher at between US$0.10 and US$0.12 in 2014. Improved border processes and management have assisted here, although there are still delays. Transporting goods through the Chirundu border between Zimbabwe and Zambia is apparently much faster than through Nakonde from Tanzania. There have been significant improvements at Chirundu over time and the border has become far more efficient over the past 20 years. From about 2009, it was already taking only two days to clear customs procedures, compared to previous years when clearance used to take up to 21 days.[25]

Rates within the domestic market tend to be higher because even though there are no borders to cross, trucking companies find it more difficult to secure return loads within Zambia, that is, along domestic routes relative to cross-border transit. Trucking company representatives commented in interviews that within Zambia, it is often a challenge to transport goods such as fertilizer to agricultural regions because there are limited opportunities for return loads if it is not harvest season. Transport rates were estimated to be between US$0.10/tonne/km and US$0.16/tonne/km for loads between major domestic centres such as Ndola, Kitwe, Lundazi and Lusaka.

In *Tanzania*, the increase in the number of trucks has led to a decrease in the transport rates from Dar es Salaam to the main local and transit destinations, to rates even below those in Zambia. For example, the transport rates from Dar es Salaam to Mbeya decreased from US$0.08 /tonne/km in 2011 to US$0.05/tonne/km in 2014, while the transport rates from Dar es Salaam to Lubumbashi in the DRC decreased from US$0.10/tonne/km in 2008 to US$0.07/tonne/km in 2013.[29] While there has been a clear decrease in the transport rates for both local and transit routes, the transport rates for the transit routes are slightly higher. ETG has its own fleet of trucks and typically factors in a cost of about US$60/tonne from Dar es Salaam to Mbeya or US$0.07/tonne/km in 2014.

Transport costs do not appear to be the reason that fertilizer prices in Tanzania remained high relative to those in Zambia in 2012 and 2013. However, there is a range of regulatory costs such as licences and permits. In particular, these include the transit goods licence (C-28 Form) from the Tanzania Revenue Authority. This licence can take several months to be issued. In one case, a truck owner's licence took roughly four months to be granted: he applied in November 2013 and the licence was issued in March 2014. It reportedly takes the longest to be issued in Tanzania compared to the other EAC countries (Kenya, Rwanda, Uganda and Burundi) where it takes only a few hours. In addition, the transit licence is reportedly the most expensive in Tanzania. The transit licence is an extremely important document because truck owners cannot travel cross-border routes without it. As a result of the licensing delay issues, it has been difficult for non-Tanzanian truck companies to enter the market, thus limiting the number of new entrants.

New entry is thus largely limited to domestic firms. This is compounded by other regulatory requirements, such as those pertaining to tri-axle heavy-load trucks, which means that firms such as TruckAfrica cannot carry a backload from Tanzania and will have to factor this into the outbound rate.[27] The effects of these regulations and logistical arrangements are that entry and competition may be constrained, even while the number of trucks in operation has increased. There is some information to suggest that new entry has been constrained by strategic behaviour on the part of powerful insiders such as trucking associations, although it is not possible to draw firm conclusions without further investigation. Some market participants advised that rates were actually set by SUMATRA. However, it appears that an 'economic rate' is calculated by SUMATRA as a benchmark to which they compare the prevailing transport rates. This benchmark is based on the operating costs that would be incurred by a brand new truck operating selected routes. SUMATRA has historically found that their benchmark rate is higher than the prevailing rates in the market, which suggests to them that the market is competitive, and as such they have not had to regulate prices in the market. The risk of using this methodology is that the benchmark is based on new trucks, whereas many of the operators in the market use second-hand and older vehicles, and that it does not take into account the efficiencies in operation that vigorous competition can bring (including organising return loads).

Another issue that affects transport rates is the arrangement between the Tanzania Truck Owner's Association (TATOA) and the Tanzania Revenue Authority, which dictates that in order to get a licence a truck owner must be a member of the industry association. Despite this, the feedback from the interviews suggests that TATOA does not set transport rates in the market nor does it wield very strong influence in the market, although it has a broad membership of approximately 900 companies. TATOA does, however, have the power to have a truck owner's licence revoked by the Tanzania Revenue Authority if certain TATOA regulations are breached, suggesting that it does wield a certain level of influence in the Tanzanian trucking industry.

In *Malawi*, there continues to be extensive regulation of road freight, which is compounded by additional regulations that apply to the transport and storage of fertilizer. The country still enforces the rules covering cabotage and the third-country rule, as does Zambia. However, it is the impact of the regulations that reveals very different outcomes with Zambia, another landlocked country. Zambia has improved the working of the regulations such that the market has effectively become contested by regional trucking operators, resulting in substantially lower transport costs.

Overall, it was estimated that more than 20 to 30 transport companies could be used by fertilizer suppliers in Malawi in 2014, but the market has been effectively dominated by a very few large players.[28] This is the case for customers who need large consignments of goods, such as sugar, tobacco or cement, need to deal with haulage companies that provide reliable and flexible service (TAG 2007: 18). Some estimates put the current combined share of the three largest road freight operators – Combine Cargo, SDV Bolloré and Manica – at between 55% and 70%.[29] SDV Bolloré is part of the global Bolloré group, which does freight forwarding and has a large fleet of trucks operating across southern and East Africa. Manica is a regional trucking group across southern Africa and is part of the South Africa Bidvest group. There are also forwarding companies that operate in the same space with some of these clearing agents also having trucks. For example, Combine Cargo is a Malawian company, but with a fleet of only 10 to 15 trucks. As its core business is freight forwarding, it normally outsources transportation services.[30]

The Road Transport Owners' Association (RTOA) is an important role player in the domestic market. While it is not compulsory to be a member of RTOA, the association does give an indication to the market of what rates should be charged in the domestic market. This raises concerns about dampening competition and providing a focal point around which domestic players can coordinate.

In addition, the Malawian government's Farm Input Subsidy Programme (FISP) identified specific truckers, on an annual basis, to transport subsidised fertilizer. Only truckers who had been appointed to provide transport for the programme via a bid could do so. Ultimately, individual trucking companies placed bids in a tender process, with the most appropriate bids being awarded contracts. The issuing of these contracts may also have had an effect on the overall outcomes in the domestic freight transport market in Malawi, particularly in scenarios where the price as set by government was seen as a pricing point on which other market participants could base their prices.

Local rates have been much higher than cross-border rates, as reflected in a number of studies (see, for example, IFDC 2013b). This is likely to be a result of the factors identified, including the weak competition in the domestic transport market and the impact of RTOA in setting recommended rates for the domestic market. There have also been higher costs than in neighbouring countries, such as for fuel and spare parts, as well as poor road conditions (IFDC 2013b: 32).[31] An empty return load has also been more likely when transporting goods within Malawi than across Malawi's borders, while backhauls from Malawi are also less likely than from other countries. Finally, domestic routes in Malawi are generally much shorter than international routes and have had much lower average loads implying higher fixed and transaction costs (AFDB 2009: 53). These factors mean that only a few transport service providers have entered the market, charging disproportionately higher prices to cover fixed costs and maximise mark-ups (Lall et al. 2009: 2).

Different estimates placed the rate for international shipments to and from Malawi at US$0.06–0.09/tonne/km (IFDC 2013b) compared with an average rate for domestic transport estimated in 2008 at US$1.63/tonne/km (AFDB 2009). The Malawi rates for cross-border transport have not been out of line with those for the other countries. Although, it is noted that the price of transporting fertilizer depends on the season and also on the availability of backhaul for the transporter (IFDC 2013b: 31). Also, while the local transport rates in Malawi appeared substantially higher, the rates offered by the Agricultural Development Marketing Corporation (ADMARC) for the domestic transportation of fertilizer for the subsidy programme was K35/tonne/km, which is approximately US$0.10/tonne/km, while transporters were demanding between K45 and K50 (between US$0.13 and US$0.14) in order to break even.[32] The Competition and Fair Trade Commission of Malawi (CFTC) launched an inquiry in 2014 into the transport sector including the trucking industry due to high transport costs being a driver of high trade costs in Malawi (Katungwe 2016).

Port efficiency is another factor that has made a substantial difference for Malawi. The closest port of Beira has a relatively low docking capacity, at between 10 000 tonnes and 15 000 tonnes. This means that only a few vessels at a time can be offloaded, leading to congestion and delays, which in turn result in demurrage charges being incurred (IFDC 2013b: 31). While Nacala has a higher docking capacity and is the closest to Lilongwe, it has been plagued by slow operations and a slow rail service. As noted above, after 2009, imports returned to being predominantly sourced from South Africa, which placed Malawi on the same footing as Zambia.

Fertilizer subsidy programmes

Fertilizer subsidy programmes have accounted for substantial volumes of fertilizer supplied to farmers in each of the countries. However, the mechanisms used to implement programmes may undermine their impact and the programme can be subject to manipulation. For example, the allocation of volumes under the subsidy programme to certain suppliers can give them an advantage in the market (as seems to have happened in Zambia, with cartel conduct having been uncovered between the two main suppliers to the subsidy programme). In the case of Malawi, the subsidy has been set so high that it seems to have set a price floor and had the effect of supporting higher overall prices, including for the substantial proportions of fertilizer that are not subsidised.

The Tanzanian subsidy programmes have historically aimed to address the higher transport costs that result in higher prices in rural areas further from Dar es Salaam. However, over time, the amount of the subsidy and the geographic reach have increased to effectively cover the whole country. At the same time, there are questions about whether it is having the desired effect of increasing fertilizer use. In all countries it is also important to note that the subsidy programmes have operated alongside the substantial commercial market supply.

Malawi

Given the importance placed on Malawi's agricultural sector, the government has aimed (through the Malawi Growth and Development Strategy – MGDS II) to increase agricultural growth by 6% and to ensure that its budget allocation to the agricultural sector has been at least 10%. In order to meet the 6% growth target by 2016, Malawi has aimed to increase fertilizer consumption from 297 000 tonnes to 600 000 tonnes annually by 2016, largely through the subsidy that makes it more affordable (IFDC 2013b: 37).

Over the years, Malawi has implemented numerous subsidy programmes: from the mid-1970s to the early 1990s, there was a universal fertilizer subsidy that subsidised smallholder credit and controlled maize prices (Dorward & Chirwa 2011: 234); from 1998/99 to 1999/00 free starter packs were issued to all households; and from 2000/01 to 2004/05 free starter packs were given to smaller targeted households. In 2005/06, the Malawian government implemented the latest subsidy programme, (the Agricultural Input Subsidy Programme (AISP), also known as the FISP), which ran until at least 2014. The large-scale input subsidy programme was a response to the persistence of food security concerns despite the earlier programmes, and it has been credited with significantly increasing fertilizer usage (Chirwa & Dorward 2013; IFDC 2013b).

The programme was facilitated by the ADMARC and the Smallholder Farmers Fertilizer Revolving Fund of Malawi (SFFRFM), the state agencies tasked with distributing fertilizer for this subsidy programme. The SFFRFM issued a competitive tender for the importation of fertilizer and for its transportation to the ADMARC warehouses (IFDC 2013b).

In terms of the programme, the district agricultural development officers from the Ministry of Agriculture and Food Security selected the beneficiary farming families. They received fertilizer, maize and legume seed vouchers. Farmers received two vouchers each, one for 50 kg of urea and another for 50 kg of NPK. Farmers redeemed the vouchers from the ADMARC/SFFRFM unit markets and farmers 'topped up' with a payment of MK500 per bag (about US$1.30) of fertilizer for both the urea and the NPK content. In 2012/13 the vouchers included security features to prevent the production and distribution of fake vouchers. In 2013/14, e-vouchers were introduced as a pilot programme in certain regions, albeit for seed only (Logistics Unit 2013, 2014).

Between 2012/13 and 2013/14, the target for FISP was around 150 000 tonnes. The farmers' contributions to the purchase of subsidised fertilizer, however, decreased dramatically over the course of the programme, which ran between 2005/06 and 2014/15. (The farmers' contributions are the amounts that farmers need to pay to top up, reflecting the difference between the price and the value of the voucher (Chirwa & Dorward 2014)). In 2005/06, the MK950 that farmers paid represented roughly 37% of the price of a bag of fertilizer and this dropped to approximately 3% in the 2012/13 season. As Malawi prices have been some 20–25% above the study's benchmarks for competitive prices, the voucher value has been substantially more than a competitively priced bag of fertilizer. This implies that the high value of the voucher may have acted as a price floor below which fertilizer would not be sold, whether to farmers with vouchers or for commercial (non-subsidised) sales. Even if there was increased competition in fertilizer trading or improvements in the cost of road transportation, the potential pro-competitive effects in the market would be muted by the price floor.

The FISP has been criticised for only meeting 47% of potential needs for increased crop production (IFDC 2013b: 19). The programme has also been criticised for a lack of transparency in the allocations of beneficiaries at the district level and administrative problems in the distribution of paper vouchers (Logistics Unit 2013). In terms of transporters, there was reportedly a lax tender process for the acquisition of transport services. Moreover, there were incidents of fertilizer theft, reflected in the 3.2% of unaccounted fertilizers (Logistics Unit 2013).

While companies are likely to submit very competitive bids in terms of low transport rates, this may be at the expense of quality (also see Ward & Barreto 2011). For example, some of the transporters did not have enough vehicles and others were used even though they were not roadworthy, for example, without speedometers or odometers. By regulating the number of truck companies the programme distorted the process of competitive rivalry between these operators, which would naturally marginalise or force less efficient and unreliable operators out of the market.

The effect of the price floor in fertilizer trading also means that there is no incentive for traders and transporters to innovate, improve quality of service, and invest in strategies to reduce their costs and thus pricing below this level. This has the effect of dampening competition in both of these levels of the market. In this way, dynamics in the subsidy programme have affected outcomes in fertilizer trading and road freight.

Tanzania

Fertilizer usage has been (and remains) very low in Tanzania, with only 9 per cent of farmers recorded as regularly using fertilizers in 2008 (Benson et al. 2012: 1). This has been attributed to a number of factors including cost, lack of sufficient knowledge about the proper use of fertilizer, and insufficient credit markets. There has been much emphasis on the fertilizer subsidy, as the government has made sustained efforts to increase fertilizer usage, particularly in rural areas and areas where there is poor road infrastructure that can sometimes be neglected by private importers.[33] The government has historically viewed agriculture as the backbone of the economy and the increased usage of agricultural inputs as critical to increasing output and ensuring security in food supply. In order to achieve this, the government has concentrated its efforts on supplying fertilizer to the major agricultural districts such as Mbeya, Iringa, Ruvuma and Rukwa, which together consume over 50% of fertilizer in Tanzania.[34]

There have been a number of fertilizer subsidy programmes in Tanzania, dating back to the 1970s: in the 1970s, the subsidy programme funded the difference between factory costs of locally produced fertilizer and its selling price; and in the 1980s, the subsidy covered the full cost of transport from the warehouse to the wholesaler/retailer.

In 2003, the subsidy was provided to wholesalers to cover the transport costs to remote areas and a portion of the final price. This policy, which was in force between 2003 and 2007, was intended to ensure that the price of fertilizer was the same throughout the country, although it also resulted in significant leakages of fertilizer to other countries.[35] The programme was based on an allocation system whereby fertilizer companies were told to deliver fertilizer to certain areas and at certain volumes, including price enforcement mechanisms to ensure reduced fertilizer prices for farmers (Benson et al. 2012: 8). In terms of the system, the government would ask the traders how much fertilizer they had in order to place orders and include the firm in the scheme, which created incentives for the companies to overstate their volumes (capacity) in order to win contracts from the government.[36]

The current subsidy programme is known as the National Agriculture Input Voucher Scheme (NAIVS) and was launched in 2008. This programme benefited from World Bank support between 2009 and 2012, which increased the number of vouchers and beneficiaries, and allowed the programme to cover the whole country (except Dar es Salaam) with the same budget input from government.[37]

The subsidy schemes in Tanzania have generally been focused on subsidising the cost of transport of fertilizer to reduce the delivered price of fertilizer across the country. As with Malawi, the scheme was expanded substantially, at least until 2014, but apparently without the concomitant increase in impact. In the case of Tanzania, the coverage was extended to the whole country. Unlike the previous subsidy scheme, the NAIVS has been targeted directly at subsidising farmers (only those with one-acre farms) rather than transportation or specific retailers. Farmers have received vouchers for two bags of fertilizer – one for planting and one for top dressing – with the value of the voucher being approximately 50% of the price of an input pack from any agro-dealer. The level of the subsidy (value of the voucher) in 2014 varied across the country: for example, in Mbeya the planting voucher carried a value of TSh50 000 and the top dressing voucher TSh40 000 (about a value of US$26–27), while in Iringa and Mtwara (somewhat closer to Dar es Salaam) the value of the voucher were TSh40 000 and TSh30 000, respectively. For planting, two types of fertilizer were authorized, namely Minjingu Mazao and DAP, although the government recommended two bags of Minjingu Mazao at TSh65 000 instead of one bag of DAP because Minjingu Mazao is produced locally. This apparently caused a reduction in the imports of CAN to Tanzania from 2012 to 2014 because it was not recommended by the government[38], which in itself distorted competitive market dynamics by affecting demand in the market. For top dressing the government authorised urea.

There was no tender process for fertilizer companies wanting to supply under the voucher system. Instead, the government issued a circular listing all the firms that had applied (through the Tanzania Fertilizer Regulatory Authority (TFRA)) and that would be allowed to participate in the programme for that year. All firms could apply to be a supplier and the TFRA issued the rights to participate on the basis of factors such as the ability to supply the products. These major companies typically had agro-dealers and agents spread throughout the country. Through these agents, the system required fertilizer companies to go to the district office (one of 109 districts) in the local area in which they wanted to participate and apply for approval to supply fertilizer to the subsidy programme in that region. The district office could refuse access to a particular supplier if, for instance, that supplier did not perform well in terms of reliability in the previous season. This placed a significant level of power in the hands of the leadership of each district, particularly in significant farming areas.

Once the agro-dealers and agents were identified, government dispersed vouchers to regions and districts through local officials to the farmers themselves. The agents and agro-dealers then competed for farmers to purchase fertilizer from them using the vouchers. The vouchers were then redeemed by the sellers through the banks, who forwarded them to government for payment. The redemption payment was either made directly to the agents or to the main fertilizer company, who then paid the agent depending on the contractual arrangement. The nature of the system was such that it was not possible to redeem a voucher designated for one district in another district, meaning that a farmer could not go and purchase fertilizer in another region where it would be cheaper, for instance.

The volume of fertilizer covered by the subsidy scheme ranged between 140 000 tonnes and 201 000 tonnes, from 2009 to 2014. This appears to be a substantial proportion of the fertilizer used (around 40%), given that import data from the Tanzania Revenue Authority showed that in 2013, imports of urea for local use (after allowing for re-exports) were just 138 522 tonnes and total fertilizer imports (including re-exports) were close to 400 000 tonnes. However, the government claimed that subsidised fertilizer was a relatively small proportion of total fertilizer used, at around 10–15% of the total market.[39] This would put the total market at a much larger size than recorded in the import data (and taking into account Minjingu's local production), suggesting that far fewer tonnes of fertilizer were actually being purchased with vouchers than were being recorded.

Zambia

Both commercial and subsidised fertilizer has been central to Zambia's Comprehensive Africa Agricultural Development Programme (CAADP). To meet the agricultural growth targets under the CAADP, implemented in 2009, fertilizer consumption in Zambia would have needed to double in just a few years (IFDC 2013a). However, outcomes in terms of the subsidy programme have been distorted by apparent cartel conduct at the level of fertilizer trading.

The Zambian government has used around 60% of the agricultural budget on two programmes for facilitating the growth in fertilizer uptake (IFDC 2013a: 2). First, the Food Reserve Agency (FRA) purchased maize 'at pan-territorial prices that are fixed above prevailing market prices'. Between 2004 and 2010, this programme purchased between 36% and 86% of all marketed maize in Zambia. By selling this maize to millers at subsidised prices millers would be expected, in turn, to sell maize products to consumers at favourable prices, protecting consumers somewhat from high prices. However, it seems that, instead, the main outcome of the programme was that it mainly benefited large-scale farmers with surplus maize sales.

The second is the Fertilizer/Farmer Input Support Programme (FISP), which has distributed subsidised fertilizer. By focusing solely on maize, the FISP has encouraged an increase in the area under maize at the expense of other crops. Large farmers with significant land resources have benefited more than small farmers (IFDC 2013a). The FISP primarily distributed D-compound and urea, and accounted for approximately 200 000 tonnes in 2013. In terms of the tender process to procure participants in the programme, the FISP Implementation Agency decided on the amount of the subsidy and asked for tenders from importers. Bids would then be selected based on a number of criteria including prices. Firms would be required to have some volumes of fertilizer available in inventory during the tender period, as this would have implications for storage costs. This stage of the process took place between March and August. It generally took importers three months to transport the product to Zambia (September to November), and then four to six weeks to distribute fertilizer around the country.

At the local level, the subsidy recipients paid for the discounted fertilizer price at the bank, received a deposit slip, and then went to a local MACO (Ministry of Agriculture and Cooperatives) office to receive a letter allowing them to collect fertilizer from the nearest importer warehouse or store.

Historically, Nyiombo and Omnia have dominated the fertilizer programme, although it appears that they have done so due to tender bidding requirements that favoured incumbents and inhibited an open and competitive process. The bidding requirements had stipulated that bidders should show that they had a track record in supplying fertilizer, including the quantities provided and proof of previously awarded contracts.[40] Of course, this gave the incumbents a substantial advantage. Other requirements included a credible track record and the capacity to the deliver on the order, along with the ability to store fertilizer around Zambia. Omnia and Nyiombo dominated supplies to the FISP, although it is understood that some of the other firms, including Zambian Fertilizers and Greenbelt, have sometimes also supplied the FISP over the years since its inception.[41]

In the commercial market, the Zambian Competition and Consumer Protection Commission (CCPC) found that market shares for Omnia and Nyiombo were 40% and 34%, respectively, based on user surveys. The Commission found that collusion between Omnia and Nyiombo had taken place in the FISP tender on prices and the division of geographic markets.[42] Omnia and Nyiombo have in recent years also been linked to allegations of fraudulent relations with the government agents that are in charge of facilitating the tender process in the Zambian Public Procurement Authority and Ministry of Agriculture.[43] The Permanent Secretary of Agriculture had to intervene in the tender process for the 2012/13 period to change the clauses of the tender bidding requirements.[44]

The FISP fertilizer subsidy programme has had a significant effect on the market for the transportation and distribution of fertilizer in Zambia overall, in so far as it has driven a significant proportion of fertilizer demand. In this regard, opening up the tender and identifying and sanctioning collusion in the tender process, reinforced the moves to open up road transportation. The change in relative prices in Zambia and the fact that the market shares of the two largest firms have been eroded in recent years suggests that there has been more meaningful competitive rivalry in the market from firms such as ETG, and more competitive outcomes.

Access to the FISP tender process seems to have been critical for farmers. When government has not met import quantities or when there have been delays in delivery, farmers have still preferred to wait for the subsidised fertilizer to arrive before purchasing from the commercial market at higher prices (IFDC 2013a). Transport to the farms has been provided by government through transporters who are hired through a bidding process (IFDC 2013a: 25).

Conclusion

To understand the economic importance of competitive and efficient transport and trading to users of these services, this chapter has examined road freight services with specific reference to the transport, trading and supply of fertilizer products. This enabled the margins and costs involved in transport and supply to be measured in terms of their effect on the final product price. It was also found that the arrangements may combine access to port and storage facilities with transport, distribution and supply activities. For example, a company may have rights to terminals, warehousing and bagging facilities at the port and also own its own trucks.

Prices paid by farmers for fertilizer have been much higher (when the subsidy programmes are not taken into account) than in the sources of fertilizer such as the Middle East and Europe. For example, average prices over 2010 to 2013 have been as much as US$339/tonne to US$559/tonne higher in Zambia and Tanzania, than the Black Sea benchmark for urea. These are 100% to 150% higher than the competitive international prices. While reasonable sea freight, port charges and bagging costs can account for around US$130/tonne, even after subtracting these costs, the margins over international prices have been more US$300–US$400/tonne for Tanzania, Malawi and Zambia, meaning African commercial farmers have paid around double for fertilizer in comparison to farmers in other countries with competitive fertilizer supply.

In Tanzania and Malawi, the fertilizer prices were found to be relatively high, especially when compared to that of Zambia and imputed competitive cost build-ups. Increased competition in the truck industry in Tanzania led to a decrease in transport prices over time. However, inefficiencies and delays related to the Dar es Salaam port had the effect of raising transport rates and thus fertilizer prices. The fact that transport prices came down but mark-ups did not, taken together with the benchmark exercise, indicate that it is the market structure in the fertilizer industry which should explain the apparently high margins embodied in local fertilizer prices.

In contrast, Zambian fertilizer prices started off much higher than those in Tanzania but gradually moved to approximately the same as those in Tanzania in 2013, in spite of much more transport being required to deliver to Zambia. A number of factors explain why the Zambian fertilizer prices became much more competitive. First, there was increased investment in trucking services largely in response to domestic and regional growth. This increase in participation in the trucking sector brought transport rates down. Second, increased mining activities provided significant backhaul opportunities for transporters of fertilizer and other goods. In effect, the transport cost is shared between the importation of fertilizer (or other goods) and the exportation of copper. This reduced the transport rate that would have otherwise been paid by the importer without the backhaul. Third, the single-permit system for Zambia, South Africa and Zimbabwe made it much easier to operate across the countries. These increased efficiencies drove down transport costs such as border delays and in turn translated into lower transport prices.

In spite of all these improvements, the rates of transport costs did not come down to below those quoted in neighbouring countries. What appears more important is that the opening up of trucking and trading meant greater rivalry in fertilizer supply. There was an increase in the participation of new fertilizer traders in the Zambian market and anticompetitive conduct was addressed by the CCPC. This was reflected in the substantial decline in the market shares of the main players with the entry and growth of ETG, which is integrated into transport and logistics. The interviews in 2014 suggested that the growth of regional rivals was spilling over into cheaper prices in Tanzania.

In Malawi, a combination of regulatory restrictions, low volumes and a very tightknit group of traders and transporters together conspired to mean prices much higher than those of its neighbours. This has had a negative effect on the costs of farmers who relied on the commercial market for fertilizer. The higher fertilizer prices also had a direct effect on the cost of the fertilizer subsidy programme, given the size of the subsidy that has been provided. Indeed, far from exerting downward pressure on prices, the programme appears to have underpinned higher prices for imported fertilizer. Taken together, these factors meant that the subsidy programme was very important (given high commercial prices), while its sustainability was questionable.

There are similar questions around how the subsidy programmes have operated in Tanzania and Zambia. Rather than supporting more competitive prices for fertilizer in general, and a wide impact in terms of improved agricultural yields, the value of the subsidy increased over time for those farmers able to access it. This raised the incentives to manipulate the programme, making monitoring and appropriate targeting to those farmers who would otherwise not be able to afford fertilizer even more important. In general terms, regulations and support need to open up markets to increased participation, while cross-border cooperation is needed to improve supplies and to monitor possible anticompetitive conduct by large international suppliers.

Notes

1 This chapter draws from a study funded by the GIZ for the SADC competition committee. This study is available at http://www.competition.org.za/working-papers/. The views expressed here are those of the authors alone. The study involved a review of desktop research, collation of publicly available data and interviews with key industry participants and stakeholders. This included face-to-face interviews in Tanzania and Zambia. In addition, interviews were conducted with international companies and regional transport bodies. Much of the information in the interviews was given under conditions of confidentiality and, as such, individual interviewees are not always identified.

2 See, for example, Arvis et al. (2010), Ward and Barreto (2011), Raballand and Macchi (2008), Teravaninthorn and Raballand (2009), and Argent and Milanovic (2014).

3 See, for example, the Grain SA Fertilizer Report 2011, for South Africa.

4 The estimates indicate that transport rates alone (aside from trading margins) from ports to landlocked countries such as Zambia are as much as US$253 per tonne, which accounts for more than 30% of the price of fertilizer.

5 Competition and Consumer Protection Commission estimates in conjunction with the International Fertilizer Development Centre (IFDC), based on the number of people surveyed who were using a particular brand of fertilizer and not the total volumes of fertilizer sold in the country

6 It is not clear how these shares were estimated so closely unless the fertilizer association was collecting sales data from market participants.

7 See http://www.zambia-weekly.com/media/zambia_weekly_2013_-_wk_38.pdf. Also see CCPC (2013). Both Tanzania and Zambia have a fertilizer subsidy programme that provides roughly one-third of fertilizer into the market.

8 See http://www.zambia-weekly.com/media/zambia_weekly_2013_-_wk_38.pdf

9 See, for example: Government broadens FISP tender process 18 April 2012/10, The Post, http://www.postzambia.com/post-read_article.php?articleId=26958; and 'Corruption deal backfires' (18 December 2013), at: http://zambiadailynation.com/2013/12/18/corruption-deal-backfires/; and 'PAC questions government over Nyiombo Investments, Omnia's contracts' (25 March 2010), at: http://www.postzambia.com/Joomla/post-read_article.php?articleId=7395

10 AMITSA compiles the data by conducting surveys in the capital city as well as in towns in each of the key agricultural production areas in a country. The data reflect the national average of the list prices obtained from this network of agro-dealers who provide the information to AMITSA on a voluntary basis. Gaps in the data reflect periods when insufficient data inputs were received for those months.

11 See NAMC Markets and Economic Research Centre, Input Cost Monitoring February (2014). Available at: http://www.namc.co.za/upload/Trends-in-selected-Agricultural-input-prices-February-2014.pdf

12 There are only two data points for 2012 for Zambia, so an annual average has not been computed.

13 The 2010 data from May to December have been averaged. This corresponds with the months for which national average fertilizer prices were available.

14 In an interview with a truck company, this was the rate at which it stated that it could break even on a trip from the Copperbelt to Johannesburg.

15 Interview with freight forwarder

16 The DCG was established in 2004. Yara is also reported to be planning to open a bagging facility, which will only handle fertilizer, while DCG's platform also handles other dry bulk goods. See http://www.bloomberg.com/news/articles/2014-09-02/yara-plans-2-5-billion-gas-based-fertilizer-plant-in-africa.

17 Interview with fertilizer company

18 Interviews with fertilizer company and freight forwarder

19 Available AMITSA disaggregated monthly price data for Chimala, which is 74 km from Mbeya city (average of prices in January and March 2014).

20 This also compares with US$42/tonne for the full cost of port handling at Dar es Salaam, which includes offloading, stevedoring, bagging, de-stuffing containers, and clearing to the port gate (interview with Fertilizer Company A).

21 Data obtained from SUMATRA

22 Interviews with trucking companies

23 Interview with SUMATRA

24 Interviews with truck companies

25 Interview with freight forwarder

26 According to SUMATRA (2011), and interviews with trucking companies for 2014 rates

27 Interview with TruckAfrica

28 Interviews with STACO and Combine Cargo

29 Interview with Combine Cargo

30 Interview with Combine Cargo

31 According to *The Nation*, the RTOA is also reported to have requested government to consider a waiver on spare parts and equipment 'so that they compete favourably with their counterparts in the region'. Transporters want spare parts waiver, *The Nation*, 13 March 2013. Accessed May 2014, http://mwnation.com/transporters-want-spare-parts-waiver

32 According to *The Nation*, Transport costs choke Admarc, *The Nation*, 16 March 2013. Accessed May 2014, http://mwnation.com/transport-costs-choke-admarc/

33 According to the Tanzania Fertilizer Company

34 Interview with the Tanzania Fertilizer Company

35 Interview with Ministry of Agriculture in Tanzania

36 Interview with the Tanzania Fertilizer Company

37 Interview with the Tanzanian Ministry of Agriculture

38 Interview with the Tanzania Fertilizer Company

39 Interview with the Tanzanian Ministry of Agriculture

40 See: Government broadens FISP tender process, *The Post*, 18 April 2012. Accessed July 2014, http://www.postzambia.com/post-read_article.php?articleId=26958

41 See: Corruption deal backfires, *Daily Nation*, 18 December 2013. Accessed July 2014, http://zambiadailynation.com/2013/12/18/corruption-deal-backfires/. Losing bidders will sell under competitive commercial market conditions parallel to the subsidy programme.

42 See: CCPC Competition and Consumer Protection News Issue 6. Accessed July 2014, http://www.ccpc.org.zm/?wpfb_dl=9. Also see Zambia Weekly. Accessed July 2014, http://www.zambia-weekly.com/media/zambia_weekly_2013_-_wk_38.pdf. The case was still under appeal in 2015.

43 See, for example: Government broadens FISP tender process, *The Post*, 18 April 2012. Accessed July 2014, http://www.postzambia.com/post-read_article.php?articleId=26958; Corruption deal. Backfires, *Daily Nation*, 18 December 2013. Accessed July 2014, http://zambiadailynation.com/2013/12/18/corruptiondeal-backfires/; PAC questions govt over Nyiombo Investments, Omnia's contracts, *The Post*, 25 March 2010. Accessed July 2014, http://www.postzambia.com/Joomla/post-read_article.php?articleId=7395.

44 See: Government broadens FISP tender process, *The Post*, 18 April 2012. Accessed July 2014, http://www.postzambia.com/post-read_article.php?articleId=26958

References

Adamopoulos T (2011) Transportation costs, agricultural productivity, and cross-country income differences. *International Economic Review* 52(2): 489–521

AfricaFertilizer.org (2012) *Training manual on fertilizer statistics in Africa*

African Development Bank (AFDB) (2009) *Malawi country economic memorandum. Seizing opportunities for growth through regional integration for trade.* AFDB Report No. 47969-MW

Argent J & Milanovic M (2014) *Rwanda's road freight industry competitiveness study.* Report prepared for TradeMark East Africa, 17 March 2014

Arvis J, Raballand G & Marteau J (2010) *The cost of being landlocked: Logistics costs and supply chain reliability.* Washington, DC: World Bank

Benson T, Kirama SL & Selejio O (2012) *The supply of inorganic fertilizers to smallholder farmers in Tanzania.* IFPRI Discussion Paper No. 01230

Chirwa E & Dorward A (2013) *Agricultural input subsidies: The recent Malawi experience.* Oxford: Oxford University Press

Chirwa E & Dorward A (2014) *The implementation of the 2012/13 farm input subsidy programme.* FISP policy brief 2014/2

Competition and Consumer Protection Commission (CCPC) of Zambia (2013) *Competition and Consumer Protection News* 6: 9

Dorward A & Chirwa E (2011) The Malawi agricultural input subsidy programme: 2005/06 to 2008/09. *International Journal of Agricultural Sustainability* 9(1): 232–247

Gregory DI & Bumb BL (2006) *Factors affecting supply of fertilizer in sub-Saharan Africa.* World Bank Agriculture and Rural Development Discussion Paper 24

Guo Z, Koo J & Wood S (2009) Fertilizer profitability in East Africa: A spatially explicit policy analysis. Prepared for the International Association of Agricultural Economists Conference, Beijing China (16–22 August 2009)

International Fertilizer Development Centre (IFDC) (2013a) *Zambia Fertilizer Assessment*

International Fertilizer Development Centre (IFDC) (2013b) *Malawi Fertilizer Assessment*

Katungwe F (2016) Competition assessment in Malawi transport sector. Paper prepared for Annual Competition and Economic Regulation (ACER) Conference Livingstone Zambia (11–12). Accessed May 2016, http://static1.squarespace.com/static/52246331e4b0a46e5f1b8ce5/t/56f1352c22482e727503e388/1458648367884/Fexter+Katungwe_+Competition+in+transport+in+Malawi.pdf

Lall SV, Wang H & Munthali T (2009) *Explaining high transport costs within Malawi: Bad roads or lack of trucking competition?* World Bank Policy Research Working Paper No. 5133

Logistics Unit (2013) *Final implementation report of the agricultural inputs subsidy programme (2012–13)*

Logistics Unit (2014) *Final implementation report of the agricultural inputs subsidy programme (2013–14)*

Meeuws R (2004) *Zambia – Trade and transport facilitation audit.* NEA Transport Research and Training, Rijswijk

Ngowi HP (2013) Impacts of removal of fertilizer value-added tax (VAT) on fertilizer use and productivity in Tanzania. Presented at the Tanzania Soil Health Policy Action Node Stakeholders Conference, Dar es Salaam (28–29 November 2013)

Raballand G & Macchi P (2008) *Transport prices and costs: The need to revisit donors' policies in transport in Africa.* BREAD Working Paper No. 190

Raballand G, Kunaka C & Giersing B (2007) *The impact of regional liberalization and harmonization in road transport services: A focus on Zambia and lessons for landlocked countries.* World Bank Africa Transport Department Policy Working Paper No. 4482

Surface and Marine Transport Regulatory Authority (SUMATRA) (2011) *Report on truck freight rate charges*

Tanzania Ports Authority (2012) *Annual report and accounts for the year ended 30 June 2012*

Teravaninthorn S & Raballand G (2009) *Transport prices and costs in Africa: A review of the international corridors.* Washington, DC: World Bank

The Alliance Group (TAG) (2007) Competition issues in the transport sector in Malawi. Report prepared for the Competition and Fair Trade Commission of Malawi

UNCTAD (2009) *Economic development in Africa report 2009. Strengthening regional economic integration for Africa's development.* New York and Geneva: United Nations

UNCTAD (2013) *Economic development in Africa report 2013. Intra-African trade: Unlocking private sector dynamism.* New York and Geneva: United Nations

Ward N & Barreto E (2011) *Technical report: Road freight transport services diagnostic study.* USAID Southern African Trade Hub

6 *Conclusions and key implications*

Alan Mlulla and Simon Roberts

As indicated in the introduction, the four sectors studied here are all important in their own right. The sectors are different in many ways and each chapter can be seen as a stand-alone contribution. However, this would be to miss out on rich cross-cutting insights which can be gained when considering them together. In addition, the assessments point to implications for competition enforcement across countries and how competition policy interacts with regional integration and economic development.

Three of the studies relate to the linked development of agricultural production and the agro-processing industry. This is one of the most important areas for Africa's economic development. Sugar is one of the longest-established cash crops in countries such as South Africa and Zambia, where there is large-scale competitive production. The industry is also highly concentrated at the level of sugar milling in some countries, where prices in domestic markets have varied substantially, reflecting the apparent exertion of market power as well as the effects of regulation. The study of poultry further illustrates the importance of vertical linkages, from agricultural production into agro-processing, and competition at different levels in the value chain. In poultry, animal feed (mainly from maize and soya) is the most important cost, with the large companies being vertically integrated backwards into feed production and horizontally across countries in southern Africa. While coordination is required to support the major investments that are necessary for expanded production, this can lead to the undermining of smaller participants.

Both sugar and poultry have generally been growing across the countries, but the underlying competitiveness depends on inputs to primary agriculture. Fertilizer is the single biggest input to commercial agriculture. The high prices of fertilizer, which have been driven partly by anticompetitive conduct as well as transport costs, have undermined the competitiveness of commercial agriculture and remain a significant obstacle to the development of the sector in African countries.

The chapter on cement also addresses a product that is important as it is an input for other activities, in this case infrastructure and housing. Here as well, anticompetitive conduct has raised prices and thus costs across the economy, which has the effect of undermining a country's ability to grow.

In this final chapter we draw together the conclusions emerging from the chapters and explore key implications. We start by considering the broad insights from the studies for competition at the regional level. This highlights the nature of rivalry, the role of lobbying by incumbents to undermine rivalry, the importance of supporting entry, and the participation of small and medium enterprises. We then reflect on the role of enforcing competition law in addressing these issues before assessing the relationship with industrial policies, and discuss proactive measures to reduce barriers to entry. The chapter concludes by drawing together key considerations for a way forward, which recognises the regional nature of rivalry and the links with regional integration and the development of productive capabilities in African economies.

Cross-cutting conclusions: Understanding competition at the regional and international levels

The major firms in all the sectors have a regional and, in some cases, a global reach. A range of relationships and structures governs their operations, including joint ventures, strategic alliances, technology agreements and trading arrangements. What cannot be in doubt is that the internationalisation of business is continuing apace and appreciating this is critical for an understanding of the conduct of large firms. An analytical framework, which is national in scope, simply cannot yield a comprehensive understanding of the competitive dynamics at play.

In some cases, the origins of the firms themselves illustrate that when it comes to the industries studied here, the internationalisation is a return to an earlier era of colonial economies that saw the construction of regional infrastructure, large agricultural estates and processing plants, and heavy industries such as cement. The roots of Illovo Sugar stretch back to this time and history has come full circle with the firm's acquisition by Associated British Foods. Most of the major cement companies are multinational corporations of European origin, although the industry has also seen significant recent entry, such as Nigeria's Dangote Cement.

In the poultry industry, global firms provide the intellectual property in the form of the high-performing breeds, while the animal feed requires sourcing grains in which international traders are increasingly involved across the region. The poultry production itself in southern Africa is led by three regional firms with various international relationships. The case of fertilizer is somewhat different as the products are almost entirely imported into the countries studied. The chapter highlighted the important linkages of supply with trading and logistics, which again are regional and international in scope.

The substantial investments required to expand competitive productive capacity, coordinated along the value chain, signifies that it is natural for large firms to be at the centre of output growth. The minimum efficient scale in industries such as cement production and sugar milling are very large relative to the size of smaller African national economies. This implies that levels of concentration will be high. The size of investments required for local industrialisation signifies that there will inevitably be a relationship with the state and this raises critical questions about whether protection is provided for those investing. Moreover, the linkages with agricultural policies in the case of sugar, as with poultry, are important for the competitiveness of the activities, as we explore below.

The studies point to the importance of competitive rivalry in disciplining the market power in concentrated industries. Four key insights emerge from the chapters.

First, competitive rivalry at a regional level, through regional trade, can be a critical source of competitive discipline, while anticompetitive coordination between firms can be aimed at preventing this. Competition markets cannot simply be defined along national borders. Following well-established principles of market definition in competition law, the definition of relevant markets needs to take into account the sources of production and locations of consumption, together with transport costs, trade flows and relative prices over time.

Second, lobbying by firms to protect small local markets likely means high prices to local consumers, including downstream industries, and undermines regional integration. Barriers to entry can also be raised through regulations that favour incumbents. While regulations may indeed be necessary, such as to ensure that proper standards are adhered to, incumbent large firms do have an interest in pushing for regulations that are crafted in a way that protects them and handicaps others. The sheer size of the incumbent firms in many of these industries and the financial and analytical resources at their disposal signifies that strong lobbying is likely. Some of the studies specifically point to concerns around regulation stifling competition. It is imperative that competition authorities and other stakeholders counter this with effective advocacy to demonstrate the value of competition and to ensure increased entry and participation in the economy.

Third, as economies grow, there is scope for new entrants and so addressing the various barriers to this is important. However, if the new entrant in one country is simply the dominant firm from a neighbour, this will not lead to lower regional concentration and greater competition. This kind of regional expansion has been demonstrated in the case studies. Instead, industrial policy has an important role to play in supporting entrants that will bring greater effective rivalry. For example, development finance can be part of opening up sectors to greater participation if it supports a number of local rivals. This is very different from a position where industrial policy supports individual national champions (who can be too big to fail) and is set against competition.

Fourth, there are opportunities for smaller firms to participate at different levels of the industry supply chains. For example, in the poultry industry, small growers can be competitive in rearing broilers if they can access competitively priced feed and breeding stock. There are smaller and local manufacturers of concrete products and suppliers of ready-mix concrete in the cement industry. In the sugar industry, the agricultural producers include out-growers and small farmers, while the users of sugar include confectionery manufacturers. Also, the supply of fertilizer can involve a host of testing and advisory services on the appropriate products for the soil, climate and crop type, while the farmers as users are perhaps the most important small-scale producer constituency in countries such as Tanzania, Malawi and Zambia, which were also the subject of the study. The ability of such firms to compete depends on vigilance in competition enforcement to ensure that the large firms with market power do not abuse their position.

There are many possible anticompetitive arrangements that can undermine the development of these industries. The most obvious and harmful are likely to be cartel arrangements. Firms that should be competing instead reach an understanding by which they maintain high prices and divide markets and consumers among themselves. Instead of consumers benefiting from vigorous rivalry between suppliers to offer keener pricing, better service and improved products for their needs, the consumers are effectively captive to one or two suppliers, even while they may not realise it themselves. These industries share many features, which create fertile ground for collusion. They are concentrated and tight-knit oligopolies of firms who know each other well, and the products are relatively homogenous. Moreover, the harm from supra-competitive pricing is huge. Cement and fertilizer are critical inputs for infrastructure and agriculture, while sugar and poultry are important consumer goods.

The benefits of competition can be seen in the pattern of cement pricing in Botswana, Namibia and South Africa after the ending of the cartel across these countries and new entry, such as by Ohorongo Cement in Namibia. By comparison, Zambia, which has had a single dominant firm, has experienced very high prices, and a rise in the cost of housing and infrastructure across the board. The study suggests that low levels of regional competition have underpinned the higher prices in several of the countries studied. This is reinforced by the lower prices reported in 2015 in Zambia with the entry of Dangote, and of more competitive pricing in Kenya in 2014 following entrants in that country.[1]

In the sugar industry, it is striking that Zambia, as one of the lowest cost producers in the world and a substantial net exporter, has among the highest prices to local buyers. The assessment of the fertilizer industry shows the benefits of more aggressive competition coupled with regulatory changes that support this. Here it is Zambia that has achieved lower prices, while Malawi has remained at the upper end.

Less well appreciated are the types of anticompetitive conduct that undermine rivalry through unilateral abuse and vertical arrangements. It is important to emphasise that large firms are part and parcel of the development of the industries studied here, and thus dominance in itself is not a target. Similarly, vertical agreements often enhance industry efficiency by allowing firms to plan their input supplies, as well as distribution and retail routes to market. However, at the same time, large firms that have market power evidently have an incentive to protect and enhance their position, and exert their power to achieve higher profits. This can involve arrangements that undermine smaller rivals and new entrants. The competition authorities need to be vigilant here.

In this regard, it is important to note that the chapters in this book are based on research studies and not investigations. While the assessments highlight the main apparent problems, conclusions of contraventions of competition law would require the gathering of evidence in a formal investigation by authorities.

Implications for competition and enforcement

Competition authorities are still relatively young in the countries considered here and the demands on them are substantial (Kovacic & Hyman 2012). Moreover, they face challenges in terms of resources and institutional capacity, while the multinational corporations they come up against are the same as those being investigated in Europe and North America.

The competition cases that have been pursued have played a valuable role in revealing information on the conduct of firms in concentrated markets. In particular, the cartels uncovered in the cement and fertilizer industries have shown how firms can divide up markets across several countries, including through industry associations. The corporate leniency policy (CLP) in South Africa has played a crucial role here (see Makhaya et al. 2012). Under the policy, the first company to come forward and reveal the full nature of the cartel conduct (such that the other cartelists can be prosecuted) is not penalised.

The effectiveness of the leniency policy as a tool for uncovering regional cartels is limited in cases where the countries do not all have a similar regime. A company applying for CLP in one country may be opening itself up to prosecution in a neighbouring country where leniency is not offered. This means that regional cartels are more durable than national cartels for two reasons. First, there is less likelihood of regional arrangements being detected by national authorities operating separately from each other. Second, the incentives to apply for leniency are much less and the cartel members can have more confidence that members will not assist an investigation. The South African experience with the large number of cartels uncovered in the past decade through strong national enforcement coupled with the CLP strongly suggests that there is extensive anticompetitive conduct in other African countries which is not being detected.

As competition problems stretch across countries, the enforcement solutions are necessarily also regional in scope, including, importantly, cooperation across competition authorities and regional competition bodies. This cooperation between authorities can include exchanging insights and sharing perspectives, even while not breaching protections on confidentiality of firm-level information. Closer working relationships can be part of building a common understanding and greater consistency of legal regimes over time. Similar considerations apply in improving merger evaluations. The possible anticompetitive effects of a regional merger may only be appreciated if a regional view is adopted.

In terms of the likelihood of unilateral exercise of market power, dominance is more likely and more durable in smaller developing economies, such as most African countries. This is due to scale economies, transport costs and likely obstacles to accessing inputs and markets (Brusick & Evenett 2008; Gal 2009; Hur 2004). The standards adopted for addressing possible abuse of dominance ought to balance the probability of abuse and the likely magnitude of the harm against the dangers of over-enforcement in finding conduct to be a contravention when it is in fact justified by efficiencies and/or chilling investment (Evans 2009; Roberts 2012). More prevalent and durable dominance suggests the need for strong enforcement provided that the institutions have the capacity to undertake the necessary analysis. Competition authorities can more effectively build capacity if they work together and share experiences.

In this light, the development of regional trading blocs is a very important issue for competition enforcement, as these involve the establishment of regional competition regimes, at least in the case of COMESA and the East African Community (EAC), and larger markets. The larger markets that the blocs imply allow for greater competition, especially if accompanied by appropriate measures to support the entry and growth of rivals. They also provide for the possible consolidation of skills and capabilities in the institutions with powers across the trade blocs. In practice, the aspirations of regional integration are a long way from realisation as protectionist measures continue to hinder trade between countries. The process of developing common institutions and of countries incorporating the regional laws in their domestic body of law has also been very slow.

Barriers to entry, competition and African industrialisation

Competition enforcement can only go so far, as it is backward looking and can only address anticompetitive conduct of incumbents. It requires supportive industrial and agricultural policies that support the development of productive capabilities of competing firms and entrants, within and across countries. However, there are several examples in the chapters of policies that support local industries that have also undermined competition, at least in the short term. The sugar industry in most countries is associated with intervention and regulations. The major difference between Kenya and Tanzania, both net importers, has been the continued protection of the local industry in Kenya even from imports from its neighbours who are members of the East African Community and/or COMESA. The protection has apparently supported an inefficient and uncompetitive industry. Kenya only opened up its market to sugar from Uganda in 2015. Kenya has also protected local producers in cement. By comparison, Tanzania has used openness to imports to discipline local firms in these sectors and has seen investment in new capacity alongside relatively more competitive pricing in both of these sectors.

In the case of Zambia, transport costs act as a natural protection to a landlocked inland economy, while there has been additional protection for some industries, such as in the form of regulatory barriers to importing sugar. The evidence suggests there have also been relatively high prices in cement and poultry products. Recent information from 2015 indicates the significant entry by Dangote has meant more competitive cement prices while investments and increased competition in poultry inputs have meant lower prices of animal feed and day-old chicks compared to neighbouring countries (Ncube & Zengeni 2016). The entry of a regional supplier in fertilizer, which followed enforcement action against the two main incumbents, has opened up the Zambian market and reduced prices compared to Malawi and Tanzania.

Therefore a necessary opposition of competition and industrial policies does not exist. The point is that where industrial policies are heavily influenced by incumbents, they tend to raise entry barriers and undermine rivalry. Instead, industrial policies are essential to lower barriers to entry including through the provision of development finance and other assistance, enabling new firms to compete with incumbents who have often inherited advantageous positions (Budzinski & Beigi 2015).

An example of these issues is the role of promised infant industry protection in attracting investment into cement in Namibia, which meant a low-cost local producer, leading to increased regional competition. Protection also supported investment in the Namibian poultry industry as it did in Botswana. This illustrates how the achievement of competitive outcomes may require support for building local productive capabilities. However, there are three critical considerations: the protection provided must be time bound; the industry must have the potential to become competitive; and support should be provided to a sector, if possible, and an individual firm should not be favoured. Where an economy is so small that it is unlikely that more than one firm can achieve the scale necessary to be an efficient producer, the support needs to be conditional and openness to regional neighbours can provide effective discipline. In the case of the poultry industry in Botswana and Namibia, competitiveness in the sector depends on the ability to source low-cost animal feed, which requires imports from neighbouring countries with better agricultural conditions.

There are good reasons to intervene directly in prices where there are market failures and/or social implications. The extensive fertilizer subsidy programmes have been implemented for both of these reasons. Smallholder farmers' yields are greatly improved by the appropriate application of fertilizer, yet the problems in fertilizer markets as well as with smallholders being able to access finance, undermine their ability to purchase the fertilizer. Subsidising fertilizer to small farmers also addresses poverty and inequality by improving the livelihoods of those who are generally among the poorest. The fertilizer case, however, also indicates how such programmes can be influenced to undermine their objectives and to benefit the incumbent suppliers.

Competition analysis can play a number of important roles in more inclusive growth beyond enforcement. It can demonstrate the size of the economic costs that result from protecting incumbents, including the costs of regulations that favour incumbents. Research and analysis of markets and firms' behaviour can also make a concrete assessment of the nature of barriers to entry and the benefits of opening up markets and supporting entrants and smaller rivals in order to generate more competitive outcomes. As the studies in this book demonstrate, a detailed understanding of firms and markets also moves us away from national units of analysis to appreciate the regional dimensions of industrialisation, competition and competitiveness.

The way forward: Interrelationships between competition policy, regional integration and economic development

It is clear that competitive outcomes are more likely with effective regional integration as this means larger markets and greater rivalry. However, the regional integration project requires relatively balanced growth across countries. Support will quickly dissipate if the majority of the gains are in the larger economies and industrial centres, even if the prices charged to consumers across countries are competitive ones. This has fundamental implications for the interface of development policies (for industries and agriculture) and competition law. Development policies need to work at the regional level to realise the potential for growth through supporting investment in capabilities and to counter the natural tendency towards agglomerations of economic activity in regions that are already more advanced.

Ultimately, growing local capacities across the region in sectors where countries have dynamic comparative advantages will increase regional trade and the intensity of competitive rivalry at the regional level. However, trade and industry policies designed around incumbent producers that protect them from competition in the region are likely to be the result of lobbying and end up shielding inefficient local producers and their supra-competitive margins. Powerful incumbents are to be expected to promote their interests strongly and align them with their own country's interests in seeking to win or protect and have advantage over another. This has contributed to the limited trade within the region, whereas there are substantial opportunities for surplus producers to export their output to countries that are net importers.

The competition being realised in regional markets must encompass the quality of the rivalry and the range and location of participants, and not just the absence of constraints. It is important that firms are competing in terms of improving products and services and investing in capabilities, while governments are facilitating such investments through appropriate policies for infrastructure provision, education and training, and development finance. In this way stronger regional value chains can develop across southern and East Africa. These value chains will mean that the necessary linkages exist across production at different levels from primary goods (such as agricultural crops) through further processing and value addition to retail markets (Keane 2015). At the same time, competitive rivalry means that large firms, whether independently or through collusion, do not act as gatekeepers to secure rents through controlling the overall chains and instead support upgrading of productive capabilities along the chain.

A common competition vision is demanding of the institutions charged with enforcement and advocacy, and of the leadership and policy vision in the different countries. There are many intermediate steps, however, which include developing a shared understanding of the issues through collaborative research and engagements, along with incremental steps to support the competition institutions that are in place, nationally and regionally. This book is one small contribution in this regard.

The competition authorities are thus part of a change in mindset that needs to link with different stakeholders and move the terms of the debate to highlight the positive links between competition and inclusive growth. A major part of this shift is for governments to recognise the cost on the economy and on low-income consumers. Towards that end, competition authorities need to step up their effort towards enforcement measures by spearheading their investigatory and enforcement efforts regarding cartels and other undesirable competition conduct, while at the same time using the insights from cases to drive the advocacy point home.

Note

1 See http://allafrica.com/stories/201508101283.html; http://www.constructionkenya.com/3007/cement-prices-kenya-drop-12-year-low-fall/

References

Brusick P & Evenett S (2008) Should developing countries worry about abuse of dominant power?' *Wisconsin Law Review* 2: 269–294

Budzinski O & Beigi M (2015) Generating instead of protecting competition. In M Gal, M Bakhoum, J Drexl, E Fox & D Gerber (Eds) *The economic characteristics of developing jurisdictions*. Cheltenham, Edward Elgar

Evans D (2009) Why different jurisdictions do not (and should not) adopt the same antitrust rules' *Chicago Journal of International Law* 10(1): 161–188

Gal M (2009) Antitrust in a globalised economy: The unique enforcement challenges faced by small and developing jurisdictions. *Fordham International Law Journal* 33(1): 1–56

Hur JS (2004) The evolution of competition policy and its impact on economic development in Korea. In P Brusick, AM Alvarez, L Cernat & P Holmes (Eds) *Competition, competitiveness and development: Lessons from developing countries*. Geneva: United Nations Conference on Trade and Development

Keane J (2015) *Firms and value chains in southern Africa*. ODI/World Bank Working Paper

Kovacic WE & Hyman DA (2012) *Competition Agency Design: What's on the Menu?* GWU Law School, Public Law and Legal Theory Paper No. 2012–135

Makhaya G, Mkwananzi & Roberts WS (2012) How should young institutions approach enforcement? Reflections on South Africa's experience'. *South African Journal of International Affairs* 19(1): 43–64

Ncube P & Zengeni T (2016) The southern African poultry value chain: Regional development versus national imperatives. UNU-WIDER Working Paper (forthcoming)

Roberts S (2012) Administrability and business certainty in abuse of dominance enforcement: an economist's review of the South African record. *World Competition* 35(2): 269–296

Contributors

Taimi Amunkete is a senior researcher for the Namibian Competition Commission (NaCC). She has previously worked as a researcher for the Namibian Economic Policy Research Unit (NEPRU) where her work involved conducting economic analysis, policy and socioeconomic research. She holds a postgraduate diploma in economics for competition law from King's College London and an undergraduate degree from the University of Namibia.

Ernest Bagopi is an investigations and research analysis manager with the Competition Authority, the enforcement agency for competition law and policy in Botswana. He has held this role since 2012, and has led investigations into abuse of dominance, restrictive business practices and cartels, resulting in breaking entry barriers in sectors (in Botswana and regionally). Ernest is a chartered marketer (SA), and holds an MBA from the University of North West (South Africa), and a postgraduate diploma in economics for competition law from the University of London.

Brian Chisanga has a BSc and MSc in agricultural economics from the University of Zambia and University of Pretoria respectively. He is currently working with the Indaba Agricultural Policy Research Institute (IAPRI) in Lusaka, Zambia as a research associate. He has previously worked in various research positions in Zambia and South Africa. His research focuses on the analysis of staple food markets including agricultural trade, pricing and value chain analysis of agricultural commodities and the welfare of smallholder farmers. He has also worked on industry competitiveness and competition policy, particularly in the sugar sector.

Emmanuel Chokwe is an economist at the Bank of Zambia. At the time of writing this book chapter he was working as a research analyst at the Competition and Consumer Protection Commission of Zambia. He holds a bachelor's degree in economics and a master's in economic policy management, both from the University of Zambia.

Godfrey Gabriel is the head of competition and market research at the Fair Competition Commission (FCC), Tanzania. He has conducted competition research in various sectors of the economy in Tanzania. He has a master's of arts in statistics specialising in econometrics, from University of Dar es Salaam, Tanzania.

John Gathiaka is a senior lecturer in the School of Economics, University of Nairobi. He has published a number of articles in the European Scientific Journal and a book, Social interactions in agriculture: Concepts, measurement and applications. He is an editor and a reviewer for several international journals. John holds a PhD (economics), MA (economics), and BA Hons degree from the University of Nairobi.

Pamela Halse is a senior analyst currently working on the Health Market Inquiry at the Competition Commission of South Africa. This follows two years with the Policy and Research

Division of the Competition Commission where she worked on cases in a range of sectors. Prior to joining the Competition Commission, Pamela was an economist at the British High Commission and before that, she was a senior economist in the National Accounts Division at Statistics South Africa. She holds an MSE in finance (economic policy) from the University of London, BA (Hons) in economics from Unisa and BSc from Florida Southern College.

Josef Hausiku currently serves as a full-time researcher at the Namibian Competition Commission (since 2012) and as an acting technical advisor to the chief executive officer, a position he has occupied since November 2015. Before joining the Namibian Competition Commission in 2012, he worked as an economist at the National Planning Commission (Namibia). Josef holds a postgraduate diploma in finance (economic policy) from the University of London and a bachelor's degree in economics from the Polytechnic of Namibia (now Namibia University of Science and Technology).

Michael Nokokure Humavindu is currently deputy permanent secretary: industrialisation and enterprise development at the Ministry of Industrialisation, Trade and SME Development. Previously he served as director: economics and sector research at the Namibian Competition Commission. Prior to this he served as the manager of research at the Development Bank of Namibia and as an economist in the Ministry of Environment and Tourism in Namibia. He is currently serving on the Ministry of Environment and Tourism's Sustainable Development Advisory Committee. He also serves on the boards of Namdeb Holdings and Agribank. Dr. Humavindu holds a PhD (economics) from the University of Umeå, Sweden, an MSc (finance and investment) from Durham University, United Kingdom and an MA (economics) from Stellenbosch University in South Africa. He has also published several peer-reviewed journal articles.

Wesley Kalapula was the chief research analyst at the Competition and Consumer Protection Commission of Zambia from 2011 to 2016, where he was responsible for conducting research on cases for the Commission. He holds a BSc in agricultural economics from the University of Zambia and a postgraduate diploma in EC competition law from Kings College, London.

Junior Khumalo is the general manager for the Policy, Research and Analysis Division at the Independent Communications Authority of South Africa (ICASA). Before joining ICASA, Junior was the divisional manager for the Enforcement and Exemptions Division at the Competition Commission of South Africa. Junior has extensive competition law experience and has worked on many investigations spanning diverse markets. He holds an MA (economics) degree from Colorado State University and a BCom Hons (economics) degree from the University of Fort Hare.

Thabiso Mbongwe is an analyst in the Department of Investigations and Research Analysis at the Competition Authority of Botswana. Thabiso holds a master's in business administration (finance) from the North-West University (Mafikeng), a postgraduate diploma in economics for competition law from Kings College, London, and a BA in social sciences (economics and public administration) from the University of Botswana. Beginning her career as an auditor at the Office of the Auditor-General, she then proceeded to join the Competition Authority of Botswana in 2012.

Allan Mlulla has been the director of research, mergers and advocacy at the Fair Competition Commission (FCC) in Tanzania since August 2009. He previously worked as the head of economic studies at the FCC. He has also worked as an institutional development specialist for the Government of Tanzania between 2006 and 2007, and as a researcher with the Economic and Social Research Foundation (ESRF) in Tanzania between 2004 and 2006. He holds a PhD (economics) from the Open University of Tanzania, MSc and BSc degrees in agricultural economics from the Sokoine University of Agriculture. He also holds a bachelor of laws degree (LLB) from the University of Bagamoyo and a master of laws (LLM in corporate and commercial law) degree from the University of Dar es Salaam.

Phumzile Ncube is a PhD candidate at the University of Johannesburg and holds a PhD scholarship issued under the South African Research Chair in Industrial Development. Prior to this, she was a researcher at the Centre for Competition, Regulation and Economic Development (CCRED) between 2014 and 2016. Phumzile completed her master's in economic development at the University of Johannesburg.

George Nguruse is the competition research analyst in the Department of Competition and Market Research of the Fair Competition Commission of Tanzania. George is a holder of a master's of science in agriculture economics and bachelor of science in agricultural economics and agribusiness (Sokoine University of Agriculture).

Benson O Nyagol is an investigator in the Enforcement Division of the Competition Authority of Kenya (CAK). He has many years of experience in the field of competition law having previously been with the institution's predecessor, the Monopolies and Mergers Commission.

Stellah Onyancha is the manager, Mergers and Acquisitions Department, Competition Authority of Kenya, which position she has held from 2014 to date. Stellah holds an MA in economic policy management from the University of Ghana, Legon, BA Hons in economics and business studies from Kenyatta University, and certificates in competition policy and law, the strategic leadership development programme and the senior management course from Kenya School of Government.

Simon Roberts is a professor of economics and executive director of the Centre for Competition, Regulation and Economic Development (CCRED) at the University of Johannesburg. Simon has been an expert economic witness in a number of major competition cases in South Africa and has advised competition authorities and governments across many African countries on issues of competition and economic policy. Simon held the position of chief economist and manager of the Policy and Research Division at the Competition Commission of South Africa from 2006 to 2012. He has a PhD from the University of London (Birkbeck College), an MA from the University of East Anglia and a BA Hons from Oxford University.

Thando Vilakazi is a senior economist at the Centre for Competition, Regulation and Economic Development (CCRED) at the University of Johannesburg. He previously worked as an economist at the Competition Commission of South Africa, and has provided training and advisory services to competition authorities, regulators and private firms in various African countries. Thando is a PhD candidate (economics) at the University of Johannesburg, and holds a BBusSc (economics) and master's degree (applied economics) from the University of Cape Town.

Index

Entries are listed in letter-by-letter alphabetical order. The page references in italics indicate where you can find information in a table or figure.